APOLLO 13

A SUCCESSFUL FAILURE

LAURA B. EDGE

TWENTY-FIRST CENTURY BOOKS / MINNEAPOLIS

Twenty-First Century Books™
An imprint of Lerner Publishing Group, Inc.
241 First Avenue North
Minneapolis, MN 55401 USA

Library of Congress Cataloging-in-Publication Data

Names: Edge, Laura B., author.
Title: Apollo 13 : a successful failure / by Laura B. Edge.
Description: Minneapolis : Twenty-First Century Books, [2020] | Audience: Ages: 12 to 18. |
    Audience: Grades: 9 to 12. | Includes bibliographical references and index. |
Identifiers: LCCN 2019009210 (print) | LCCN 2019014184 (ebook) | ISBN 9781541581760
    (eb pdf) | ISBN 9781541559004 (library bound : alk. paper)
Subjects: LCSH: Apollo 13 (Spacecraft)—Juvenile literature. | Space vehicle accidents—
    United States—History—20th century—Juvenile literature. | Project Apollo (U.S.)—
    Juvenile literature.
Classification: LCC TL789.8.U6 (ebook) | LCC TL789.8.U6 A53289 2020 (print) |
    DDC 629.45/4—dc23

LC record available at https://lccn.loc.gov/2019009210

Manufactured in the United States of America
1-46286-46270-9/12/2019

1
EXPLOSION IN SPACE

MAN MUST RISE ABOVE THE EARTH, TO THE TOP OF
THE CLOUDS AND BEYOND, FOR ONLY THUS WILL HE
FULLY UNDERSTAND THE WORLD IN WHICH HE LIVES.

—SOCRATES, 399 BCE

On the evening of April 13, 1970, three astronauts floated around the Apollo 13 spacecraft in zero gravity. Jim Lovell, Fred Haise, and Jack Swigert were on their way to the moon.

THE CREW

Flight commander Lovell knew from an early age that he would make rocket science his life's work. As a boy, he read every book about rocketry he could find. In high school, with the help of his chemistry teacher and two friends, he built a rocket. The teens took it to an empty field, packed it with homemade gunpowder, and lit the fuse. The rocket blasted 80 feet (24 m) in the air, zigzagged a bit, wobbled, and exploded. Lovell was hooked.

After high school, Lovell studied engineering at the University of Wisconsin. Then he transferred to the US Naval Academy at Annapolis where he wrote his senior thesis on liquid-fuel rocketry. After graduation, he entered the naval flight-training program and became a test pilot for military jets. When the manned spaceflight program began looking for pilots to ride rockets into space, Lovell jumped at the chance to apply. The astronaut-training program accepted him.

By the time of the Apollo 13 launch, Lovell had flown three space missions and logged more hours in space than any other astronaut. He had circled the moon and seen its pale gray pits and craters outside the spacecraft window. On the Apollo 13 mission, he was getting ready to fulfill a lifelong dream—to walk on the surface of the moon.

Apollo 13 was the first spaceflight for the other members of the crew. Haise, a native of Biloxi, Mississippi, earned a degree in aeronautical engineering from the University of Oklahoma. He served with the air force as a tactical fighter pilot and test pilot and flew for the marine corps, the navy, and the Oklahoma Air National Guard.

Exploration and the science of space travel fascinated Haise. He spent many hours learning how to identify different types of

James (Jim) A. Lovell Jr., Apollo 13 Commander

rocks. He practiced operating the geological equipment the crew would use to extract rock and soil samples on the moon. Haise looked forward to the discoveries their exploration of the moon would reveal.

Swigert was a last-minute replacement for astronaut Ken Mattingly. One week before the launch, a member of the backup crew came down with German measles. Before his symptoms appeared, he unknowingly exposed the primary crew to the disease. Blood tests revealed that Lovell and Haise were immune to German measles. Mattingly's blood test was inconclusive. Possibly, he could become sick during the spaceflight. Officials at the Kennedy Space Center felt it was too risky, so backup astronaut Swigert replaced Mattingly.

Fred W. Haise Jr., Apollo 13 Lunar Module Pilot

As a backup astronaut for the Apollo 13 mission, Swigert had trained alongside the primary crew for more than a year. Mere days before liftoff, he drilled rigorously with his new crew to prepare for the flight. The highly skilled pilot got his private pilot license at the age of sixteen. His degrees in mechanical and aerospace engineering provided Swigert with the knowledge and confidence to step into his new role on short notice. His service in the air force as a fighter pilot and test pilot proved he had the steely nerves required for a trip to outer space.

John "Jack" L. Swigert Jr., Apollo 13 Command Module Pilot

Teams of engineers, scientists, and mathematicians worked at the National Aeronautics and Space Administration (NASA) Mission Control Center in Houston, Texas. They monitored every second of the spaceflight, solving problems, adjusting equipment, and helping the astronauts keep the complicated spacecraft running smoothly.

THE MISSION

The astronauts were well on their way to the moon. They planned to land Apollo 13 in a rugged, hilly area of the moon called Fra Mauro. Made up of ridges, hills, and valleys, the region interested scientists because of the variety in the landscape. Scientists hoped to gain insight into the moon's geological history from the rock samples the astronauts planned to bring back to Earth.

AN UNLUCKY NUMBER

Some people believe the number 13 is an unlucky number. In the ancient world, the number 12 was often considered the "perfect" number. The Sumerians developed a base-12 system that is still used for measuring time. A day is made up of two 12-hour periods. Most calendars have 12 months. According to this view, adding one to the perfect number is asking for trouble. Many high-rise buildings in the United States do not have a 13th floor, and many hotels, hospitals, and airports avoid using the number for rooms and gates.

So some people thought Apollo 13 was a terrible name for a dangerous flight to the moon. They wanted to call the mission Apollo 12B or Apollo 14. Anything but Apollo 13. And the digits of the launch date, 4/11/70, added up to 13. The launch was scheduled for 13:13 military time. But the astronauts didn't pay attention to the superstitious mumbo jumbo. They were highly trained professionals. They relied on science.

With two days left until the lunar landing, the pale glow of the moon loomed large outside the spacecraft windows. Mission control in Houston reported that all systems were running smoothly. "The spacecraft is in real good shape as far as we're concerned," they said. "We're bored to tears down here."

The crew filmed a television program for space fans on Earth. Lovell held a movie camera and recorded Haise as he floated around the spacecraft and pointed out different equipment that would be used on the moon. He showed the audience the backpacks they would wear on the moon. Containing oxygen and water, the backpacks kept the men comfortable as they ran scientific experiments and explored. Lovell ended the telecast with, "This is the crew of Apollo 13 wishing everybody there a nice evening."

APOLLO 13 MISSION PATCH

Astronaut crews for each space mission design their own mission patch. Typically, the patch includes the crew's names and visual elements that represent the goals of the mission. The mission patch for Apollo 13 broke with tradition by not including the astronaut's names. The design highlighted the scientific focus of the flight. It showed the sun god, Apollo, driving his chariot across the sky from Earth to the moon. Written on the patch in Latin was the motto *Ex Luna, Scientia* or "From the Moon, Knowledge." The emblem symbolized that the mission would extend Apollo's light of knowledge to all humankind.

A BIG BANG

After filming the television show, mission control passed along a few routine tasks for the crew to complete before they turned in for the night. One of those chores was to stir the oxygen and hydrogen tanks. This turned on fans in the tanks and resettled the supercold gases so they would not stratify, or form into layers. Stirring the gases from time to time made sure the quantity readings in the tanks were accurate.

Swigert flipped four switches on the instrument panel, two for oxygen and two for hydrogen.

Seconds later, the astronauts heard a loud bang. The spacecraft shook with a violent whump-shudder.

Amber warning lights flashed, and alarms sounded.

"Okay, Houston," Swigert said. "I believe we've had a problem here."

"This is Houston," replied mission control. "Say again, please."

"Houston, we've had a problem," answered Lovell.

The astronauts scanned the instrument panel, and the readings looked ominous. The spacecraft was losing oxygen and electrical power quickly.

Outside Apollo 13's metal shell was the vacuum of space, where temperatures ranged from 248°F (120°C) in sunlight to −148°F (−100°C) in shadow. There was almost no air pressure. A hole in the spacecraft could cause the astronauts' lungs to explode and their blood to boil.

This was not the first problem on a space mission. Many glitches had occurred over the years. But this was more than a glitch. The astronauts were in serious trouble.

And their dying spacecraft was 200,000 miles (321,870 km) from Earth.

2

THE RACE FOR SPACE

THE EXPLORATION OF SPACE WILL GO AHEAD, WHETHER WE JOIN IN IT OR NOT, AND IT IS ONE OF THE GREAT ADVENTURES OF ALL TIME, AND NO NATION WHICH EXPECTS TO BE THE LEADER OF OTHER NATIONS CAN EXPECT TO STAY BEHIND IN THIS RACE FOR SPACE.

—PRESIDENT JOHN F. KENNEDY

On June 3, 1965, astronaut Ed White became the first American to walk in space.

Apollo 13 was the third NASA mission to send astronauts to land on the moon. Thousands of scientists, engineers, and mathematicians worked for more than a decade to accomplish this extraordinary feat.

And it started with a race.

THE COLD WAR

After World War II (1939–1945), the United States and the Soviet Union (a former nation of republics that included Russia) saw each other as a threat. Both nations had nuclear weapons and feared an attack by the other. This period of suspicion between the United States and the Soviet Union was the Cold War (1945–1991).

The United States practiced a democratic form of government. Its economy was based on capitalism, a system where individuals and companies own goods. The Soviet Union practiced a Communist form of government. The Communist government controlled the economy. Both countries wanted to prove to the world that their form of government and economic system were the best. Landing a person on the moon was a dramatic way to accomplish that and to avoid an all-out war.

On October 4, 1957, the Soviet Union launched *Sputnik I*, the first satellite, into space. The achievement shocked the United States. It proved the Soviet Union had surpassed the US in technological skills. The US felt its national security was under threat. If the Soviets could launch a satellite into space, they could just as easily lob a nuclear bomb at the United States. The reputation of the country was in jeopardy. America had to catch up quickly.

In response to *Sputnik I*, President Dwight D. Eisenhower signed the National Aeronautics and Space Act. On October 1, 1958, NASA was formed as a civilian agency within the national government. NASA's purpose was to explore space and obtain scientific knowledge. It would develop spacecraft and create programs to launch Americans into space.

BUILDING A SPACE AGENCY

Space exploration is a complicated business, and NASA had much to learn. They had to figure out how to build a spacecraft that was safe for people to ride in, how to attach it to a rocket and blast it into space, how to keep it moving in the right direction, and how to bring it safely back to Earth. The people working at the agency were modern pioneers in the frontier of space.

German scientist Wernher von Braun and a team of rocket scientists developed rockets powerful enough to break through Earth's gravity. Rival companies in the United States competed against one another to build spacecraft that would protect astronauts from the harsh environment of space. NASA set up the Mission Control Center in Houston, and flight controllers developed procedures to make sure each phase of each mission was a success. Engineers developed computing, communications, and guidance systems to enable mission control to communicate with and assist astronauts in flight. NASA also set up tracking stations around the world. These stations would enable them to monitor the location of spacecraft from various points around the globe. These innovations were designed with computers less powerful than a Wi-Fi router.

Besides building hardware, NASA set the requirements for astronaut candidates. They began with military test pilots, which meant that all the candidates were men because women couldn't serve in the military as pilots in 1959. From that initial group, NASA outlined requirements for age, height, education, intelligence, temperament, and physical ability. The men had to be less than forty years old and less than 5 feet 11 inches (1.8 m). They had to have a bachelor's degree in engineering, science, or math. They had to be qualified jet pilots with a minimum of fifteen hundred hours flying time. And they had to be in excellent physical and mental condition.

EXPANDING THE GROUP

The first seven astronauts were all white men with experience flying jets and with training as engineers. As the space program grew, NASA modified the qualifications for astronauts to include a more diverse group. The agency now accepts applications from civilian candidates and women. In June 1983, Sally Ride became the first female American astronaut. She held multiple degrees from Stanford University, including a PhD in physics. She was a highly trained mission specialist. Guion Bluford, the first African American man in space, made his historic flight on August 30, 1983. Before joining NASA, Bluford was an air force fighter pilot during the Vietnam War (1959–1975). He flew 144 combat missions and won multiple medals for his military service. In September 1992, Mae Jemison, the first African American

Project Mercury astronauts (*clockwise from the back left*): Alan B. Shepard Jr., Virgil I. Grissom, L. Gordon Cooper Jr., M. Scott Carpenter, John H. Glenn Jr., Donald K. Slayton, and Walter M. Schirra Jr.

woman, joined the ranks of space explorers. Jemison entered Stanford University on scholarship when she was sixteen years old and earned bachelor's degrees in chemical engineering and African American studies. She went on to earn a PhD in medicine from Cornell University. Jemison served as a science mission specialist for NASA and logged more than 190 hours in space.

Candidates went through rigorous physical and psychological testing. NASA eliminated the majority for one reason or another. From a field of five hundred candidates, NASA selected only seven men to be astronauts: Gordon Cooper, Scott Carpenter, John Glenn, Deke Slayton, Wally Schirra, Gus Grissom, and Alan Shepard. According to Dee O'Hara, the medical nurse for the astronauts, "They were the best America had to offer. . . . They put their backsides on the line because it was such a new program—new everything—and they stepped up to the plate and did it."

PROJECT MERCURY

Project Mercury, America's first human spaceflight program, began in 1958. Its purpose was to send astronauts into space and test the effects of space travel on people. A series of six missions from 1961 to 1963 worked toward the goal of sending a manned spacecraft into orbit around Earth.

Before NASA launched the first human into space, it had to test the spacecraft thoroughly. Many early mishaps occurred while developing rockets and training astronauts. Many rockets blew up on the launchpad or exploded a few feet in the air. According to Guenter Wendt, a mechanical engineer for McDonnell Aircraft, the company that built the Mercury spacecraft, "We launched between fifteen and twenty

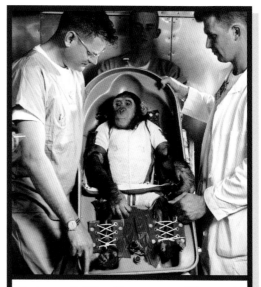

On January 31, 1961, a chimpanzee named Ham paved the way for the first American in space when he rode a Mercury-Redstone rocket on a suborbital flight and returned safely to Earth.

rockets a week, but three out of five would blow up."

With each attempt, engineers gained valuable knowledge and moved closer to their goal. By January 1961, NASA felt confident enough to launch a chimpanzee named Ham into space. After Ham returned safely to Earth, NASA went ahead with plans to send up the first human.

In spite of the risks, all seven astronauts wanted to be first to fly into space. For long hours, they trained intensely for a job no one had ever done. Shepard told a reporter, "Of course, I want to be first. The challenge is there, and I've accepted it."

Glenn agreed. "I think that anyone who doesn't want to be first doesn't belong in this program."

But the Soviet Union beat the US. On April 12, 1961, Russian cosmonaut, or astronaut, Yuri Gagarin piloted a Vostok spacecraft into Earth orbit. The US space program reeled with disappointment. The Soviet Union was ahead in the space race.

On May 5, 1961, the first American blasted into space. Shepard lifted off on *Freedom 7*, named in honor of the seven original astronauts. He flew 116 miles (187 km) high and then returned to Earth. The flawless fifteen-minute flight was broadcast around the world. When Shepard's capsule splashed down in the Atlantic Ocean, church bells rang, sirens wailed, and cheering crowds streamed into the streets in his hometown of Derry, New Hampshire. The astronaut became an instant celebrity.

Three weeks after Shepard's historic flight, Kennedy stood in front of a joint session of Congress and ignited the fire of America's space race. "I believe that this nation should commit itself to achieving the goal, before this decade is out, of landing a man on the Moon and returning him safely to the Earth. No single space project in this period will be more impressive to mankind, or more important for the long-range exploration of space; and none will be so difficult or expensive to accomplish."

With Shepard's success and the president's challenge, the US space program took off. On July 21, 1961, Grissom piloted

Liberty Bell 7. The fifteen-minute flight went smoothly—until the recovery phase. The spacecraft splashed down in the Atlantic Ocean, and Grissom waited for a helicopter to pluck him out of the water. All of a sudden, the hatch blew off and water poured into the capsule. Grissom pulled off his helmet and hurled himself into the rough sea. He swam away from the spacecraft and watched in horror as it slowly filled with water and sank. Water

On July 21, 1961, Mercury-Redstone 4 (MR-4) launched. Astronaut Gus Grissom piloted *Liberty Bell 7* on a fifteen-minute suborbital flight.

seeped into Grissom's space suit, making him heavier and heavier. "At this point the waves were leaping over my head, and I noticed for the first time that I was floating lower and lower in the water. I had to swim hard just to keep my head up."

Rescue helicopter pilots lowered a sling and hoisted the astronaut out of the sea. They flew Grissom to the USS *Randolph,* an aircraft carrier waiting nearby. As Grissom mourned the loss of his spacecraft, a ship's officer handed him his space helmet. One of the rescue pilots had snatched it out of the water near a circling 10-foot (3 m) shark.

ORBITING EARTH

As NASA worked on plans for a US spaceflight to orbit Earth, twenty-five-year-old Russian cosmonaut Gherman Titov spent a full day in space aboard *Vostok 2.* He orbited Earth seventeen times, and he was the first person to eat and sleep in space.

Discouraged but not defeated, the US space program plunged ahead. NASA selected Glenn as the first American to orbit Earth. Bad weather delayed the launch for nearly two months. On February 20, 1962, Glenn orbited Earth three times on *Friendship 7*. The flight went smoothly until a warning light flashed in mission control. The light indicated that the heat shield on *Friendship 7* had come loose. The heat shield protected the spacecraft from the intense heat of reentering Earth's atmosphere. Without it, Glenn would burn up in seconds.

Mission control considered its options. Possibly, a faulty instrument was giving the reading and the heat shield was fine. NASA had never encountered a similar problem in training exercises or previous spaceflights. An accurate warning signal could mean heat shield failure, a horrible death for Glenn, and an unrecoverable blow to the US space program. Some mission control staff felt it was an instrument error, and they should do nothing. Others thought they should try to hold the heat shield in place somehow.

Mission control decided to hold the heat shield in place by leaving the retropack (a group of rockets under the heat shield) attached to the spacecraft. Normally, the retropack was released after it fired. If mission control left the retropack attached, it might hold the heat shield in place. But the retropack could also damage the heat shield or change the trajectory, or path, of the spacecraft on reentry. The agonizing decision for mission control worked. The heat shield held, and Glenn returned safely to Earth, a new American hero. NASA later determined the heat shield was never loose. The problem was an instrument error.

Carpenter, Schirra, and Cooper also piloted Project Mercury missions. They orbited Earth and conducted scientific experiments. They performed maneuvers and tested various parts of the spacecraft. They ate and drank during spaceflights. When doctors examined each of the men upon their return, they confirmed that people could survive in weightlessness. NASA felt confident to move on to longer flights in its quest to reach the moon.

Recovering *Liberty Bell 7*

*L*iberty Bell 7 sat on the ocean floor for thirty-eight years. In
1999 a team of underwater search and recovery experts lifted
the spacecraft from the sea and hauled it aboard a recovery ship.
Transferred to the Cosmosphere, a space museum in Hutchinson,
Kansas, the capsule was carefully cleaned and restored. It is part of
the exhibit "The Lost Spacecraft: *Liberty Bell 7* Recovered."

Curt Newport (*seated*), an underwater salvage expert, led the expedition to retrieve *Liberty Bell 7*. Newport located the capsule and, after one abortive attempt, successfully raised it from the ocean floor. The recovery of *Liberty Bell 7* fulfilled a fourteen-year dream for the expedition leader.

On February 20, 1962, astronaut John Glenn entered the capsule, *Friendship 7*. He blasted into space on a Mercury-Atlas 6 rocket and became the first American to orbit Earth.

While NASA completed the Project Mercury missions, the Soviet Union launched *Vostok 3* in August 1962. A day later, they launched a second manned spacecraft. The two spacecraft orbited Earth at the same time, and *Vostok 3* stayed in space for ninety-four hours, longer than any previous flight. The Soviet government celebrated the achievement, boasting to the world's press, "Communism is scoring one victory after another in its peaceful competition with capitalism."

The US couldn't seem to catch up in the space race. On June 16, 1963, Valentina Tereshkova, a Soviet, became the first woman in space. And in March 1965, Alexei Leonov became the first person to venture outside a spacecraft in a space suit.

PROJECT GEMINI

NASA learned a great deal about spaceflight from Project Mercury. But the agency still had much to accomplish before it would be able to send people to the moon and bring them back safely to Earth.

A mission to the moon and back would take nine to fourteen days. Cooper had stayed in space for thirty-four hours on the final Project Mercury flight. NASA needed to make sure the human body could withstand the stress of spaceflight for two weeks. NASA also had to develop safe space suits so that the astronauts could walk on the surface of the moon. Finally, NASA had to find a way for two spacecraft to rendezvous, or meet and fly together, in space. One spacecraft needed to take off from the lunar surface, rendezvous with another spacecraft orbiting the moon, and return to Earth. All these goals were part of NASA's second human spaceflight program, Project Gemini, and all had to be met before NASA could attempt a lunar landing.

Valentina Tereshkova, the first woman in space, in front of the *Vostok 6* in 1963. It would take the US until 1983 to send a woman to space.

The first two Gemini flights were unmanned and tested the new Titan II rocket. Two-man crews flew ten Gemini missions in 1965 and 1966. Gemini 3 astronauts Grissom and John Young orbited Earth three times. They tested the newly designed Gemini spacecraft, its onboard computer system, and its flight crew equipment.

The fourth Gemini flight, Gemini 4, reached the goal of a four-day flight. Gemini 4 also achieved another milestone. Astronaut Ed White ventured outside the spacecraft in a space suit. During his twenty-minute space walk, White was connected to the spacecraft with a cable. Pilot Jim McDivitt flew the spacecraft and took pictures of his fellow astronaut floating above the dazzling blue Earth. "This is the greatest experience," White said. "It's just tremendous."

Project Gemini closed the gap in the space race. Gemini 5 stayed in space for eight days. In December 1965, Gemini 6 and Gemini 7 met in space and flew in formation. Gemini 7 stayed in space for two weeks. Gemini 8 successfully docked with, or connected to, another spacecraft. During Gemini 9, 10, 11, and 12, astronauts tested different ways of docking with other spacecraft. They also performed space walks of longer durations. The knowledge and technical expertise gained on Project Gemini made a lunar landing possible. NASA moved into its third phase of space exploration with a project to reach the moon. They called the project Apollo.

APOLLO TRAGEDY

The Apollo program went live in 1967. Only three years remained to land human beings on the moon by the end of the decade. Design challenges slowed progress on the three-person Apollo spacecraft, which was far more complex than Mercury or Gemini spacecraft. The Apollo spacecraft had to sustain three men for two weeks or more in Earth orbit or lunar orbit. It had to hold enough fuel for the long trip to the moon and back. And it needed a more powerful rocket to blast it into space.

On January 27, 1967, Grissom, White, and Roger Chaffee tested the launch of the new Apollo spacecraft. For more than five hours, they sat strapped inside the capsule and went through a dress rehearsal for the first Apollo launch. They noted several problems with the communications system. Mission control struggled to hear them through crackling static. As the countdown wound down, a piece of exposed wiring produced a spark. The capsule, filled with pure oxygen, burst into flames.

The astronauts struggled to open the hatch, but it wouldn't budge.

Apollo 1 astronauts Gus Grissom, Ed White, and Roger Chaffee were killed when a fire swept through the oxygenated command module during a preflight test on January 27, 1967.

"We've got a bad fire," Chaffee shouted. "We're burning up here!"

Flight controllers nearby saw a flash of bright orange light. They grabbed fire extinguishers and ran toward the inferno. But flames, thick smoke, and poisonous fumes made reaching the trapped men impossible. It took five minutes to open the hatch, and by then it was too late. The capsule looked like the inside of a furnace. All three astronauts were dead.

The Apollo 1 disaster stunned the nation. The US Senate investigated, held hearings, and made recommendations. NASA went over every inch of the spacecraft and made massive design changes. The thousands of people who worked on Apollo pledged to reach Kennedy's goal of landing on the moon. They recalled

Grissom's words from an interview one week before the tragedy. "If we die we want people to accept it. . . . We hope that if anything happens to us it will not delay the program. The conquest of space is worth the risk of life."

APOLLO TRIUMPH

NASA forged ahead with a newly designed Apollo spacecraft. Engineers called it the safest spacecraft ever built. NASA carefully tested every aspect of the new design. They launched three unmanned test flights to make sure everything worked properly. Then they tested the spacecraft with astronauts orbiting Earth, and then orbiting the moon. Finally, on July 16, 1969, NASA launched Apollo 11. Astronauts Neil Armstrong, Buzz Aldrin, and Michael Collins flew the spacecraft *Columbia* into orbit around the moon. Then, on July 20, Armstrong and Aldrin detached the lunar landing module, *Eagle*, and touched down on an area of the moon called the Sea of Tranquility. "Houston, Tranquility Base here," Armstrong said. "The *Eagle* has landed." Armstrong lowered a small TV camera and then slowly backed down the spacecraft ladder. Six hundred million people around the world watched. When he stepped onto the moon's pale gray, powdery surface, Armstrong said, "That's one small step for man. One giant leap for mankind."

Aldrin joined Armstrong a few minutes later. The astronauts planted an American flag on the moon. They conducted scientific experiments, collected rock samples, and took many photographs. They talked to President Richard Nixon at the White House. And they left behind a commemorative plaque:

HERE MEN FROM THE PLANET EARTH

FIRST SET FOOT UPON THE MOON

JULY 1969 A.D.

WE CAME IN PEACE FOR ALL MANKIND

A New View of Our Fragile World

Apollo 8's mission was to orbit the moon ten times. Its three astronauts traveled farther and faster than anyone had ever traveled. They looked out the windows of their spacecraft and, for the first time in human history, saw the moon below them. As they orbited the moon, Earth rose over the horizon. The astronauts snapped a picture of the fragile-looking blue disk floating in the black emptiness of space. They called it *Earthrise*. The photograph gave people all around the world a new appreciation for the beauty and vulnerability of Earth. One of the most famous images in history, *Earthrise* inspired many environmentalists to increase their efforts to protect our planet.

This photograph, taken from Apollo 8 as it orbited the moon, shows Earth rising over the moon's horizon. The image gave people a new view of Earth as a fragile, vulnerable planet.

Collins circled the moon in *Columbia*. The lunar explorers completed their objectives, returned to the *Eagle*, and rested. Then they blasted off the lunar surface and rejoined *Columbia* for the trip back to Earth. Four days later, the trio splashed down in the Pacific Ocean. John F. Kennedy's dream had become a reality.

Apollo 12 also landed on the moon. Astronauts Charles "Pete" Conrad and Alan Bean touched down in the Ocean of Storms. The astronauts performed two moonwalks and stayed on the lunar

Astronaut Buzz Aldrin, Apollo 11 Lunar Module pilot, poses for a photograph beside the US flag that he and Commander Neil Armstrong placed on the moon on July 20, 1969.

Astronaut Alan Bean, Apollo 12 Lunar Module pilot, prepares to step off the ladder of the lunar module and explore an area of the moon called the Ocean of Storms with the commander Charles Conrad.

surface for seven hours and forty-five minutes. They conducted experiments, brought back many rock and soil samples, and returned safely to Earth.

Then came Apollo 13. Jim Lovell and Fred Haise planned to land in the Fra Mauro highlands. Theirs was a true scientific mission, with lots of experiments planned. After the explosion on board, the astronauts weren't sure they would be able to land on the moon. They weren't even sure they'd make it back to Earth.

It was the greatest challenge the US space program had ever faced.

A Glimmer of Hope in a Dark Time

The 1960s were turbulent years for the United States. Kennedy was assassinated in 1963. The United States sent combat troops to Vietnam in 1965. The US faced civil unrest, and the battle against racial discrimination raged, sometimes violently. And then, in 1968, Dr. Martin Luther King Jr. and Senator Robert Kennedy of New York were both assassinated. The success of the US space program provided a glimmer of hope for the divided nation. The United States took the lead in the space race and surpassed the Soviet Union in technological achievements. The Apollo program demonstrated the best in US ingenuity, teamwork, and complex problem-solving. It gave

people hope. If we could send Americans to the moon and bring them safely back to Earth, maybe we could find a way to solve the many problems on Earth.

Apollo 7 was the first mission to have live television broadcasts. Mission commander Walter Schirra (*right*) holds a sign for viewers during the first live transmission. Command module pilot Donn Eisele is to the left.

[ALL FLIGHT CONTROLLERS MUST] BE AWARE THAT SUDDENLY AND UNEXPECTEDLY WE MAY FIND OURSELVES IN A ROLE WHERE OUR PERFORMANCE HAS ULTIMATE CONSEQUENCES.

—FLIGHT CONTROLLER'S CREED

The Apollo 13 spacecraft wobbled. Warning lights on the instrument panel lit up. Alarms buzzed. The astronauts had no idea which of the five million systems on the spacecraft was causing the problem. To fix it, they had to figure out what was broken.

THE SPACECRAFT

The spacecraft had three separate sections, or modules—each section for a specific job. The astronauts sat in the cone-shaped command module—the living quarters for the crew during the flight. Nicknamed *Odyssey*, the command module was the flight control center for the spacecraft. It contained gray instrument panels covered with about five hundred toggle switches, push buttons, thumb wheels, and rotary switches with click stops. Covered by a heat shield so the astronauts could withstand the high temperatures of breaking through Earth's atmosphere, the command module was the only part of the spacecraft that would return to Earth.

Connected to the bottom of the command module was the service module. This section looked like a giant tin can. It contained the main engine and the guts of the spacecraft. The service module held oxygen and hydrogen tanks. These were connected to three fuel cells. When the gases were mixed together in the fuel cells, they provided electrical power, water, and heat for the spacecraft. The oxygen tanks also contained the crew's supply of breathable air. Even though the service module and the command module were connected, the astronauts could not see into or access the service module.

The lunar module was nicknamed *Aquarius*. It looked like a four-legged spider and was the only part of the spacecraft that would land on the moon. *Aquarius* was stored inside the topmost section of the Saturn V rocket that blasted the astronauts into space. This served as a sort of garage to protect the delicate spacecraft on the turbulent ride through Earth's atmosphere. On the way to the moon, the astronauts had to pull *Aquarius* out of the top of the rocket and attach it to *Odyssey*.

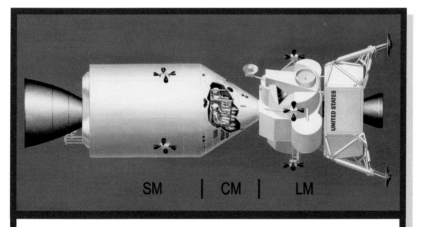

The diagram shows the size of the Apollo spacecraft and each of the modules: the service module, the command module, and the lunar module.

DOCKING *AQUARIUS* TO *ODYSSEY*

After the spacecraft was safely on its way to the moon, Jack Swigert, the command module pilot, separated the command and service modules from the Saturn V rocket. He nudged *Odyssey* forward, away from the rocket, using small bursts from *Odyssey*'s thrusters. Then he slowly turned the spacecraft around until it faced the rocket nose first. Panels on the rocket opened like a flower and revealed the lunar module *Aquarius* nestled inside. Swigert eased *Odyssey* forward, inch by inch. He lined up the probe on *Odyssey*'s nose to fit into a hole on the top of *Aquarius*. The two crafts docked, and twelve latches activated to lock the spacecraft together and form a tight pressure seal.

BLASTING INTO SPACE

For the trip to outer space, the Apollo 13 spacecraft was strapped to the top of a Saturn V rocket. Filled with more than 1 million gallons (3.8 million L) of liquid oxygen, liquid hydrogen, and kerosene fuel, the Saturn V weighed more than 3,000 tons (2,722 t). It was as powerful as an atomic bomb. This massive beast lifted the spacecraft off the ground, fought and escaped Earth's

Apollo 13 liftoff, April 11, 1970

gravity, and hurled across the sky at 17,500 miles (28,163 km) per hour.

The crew of Apollo 13 (*from left to right*): the command module pilot Jack Swigert, the commander Jim Lovell, and lunar module pilot Fred Haise.

Swigert slowly backed up *Odyssey* and gently pulled *Aquarius* out of the rocket. Separated from the spacecraft, the rocket fell away. Mission control estimated that it would crash onto the moon at about seventy-seven hours into the flight. Swigert then turned the combined *Odyssey-Aquarius* spacecraft around, so that *Aquarius* was in front, and continued the trek to the moon.

After they heard the bang and felt the spacecraft shake and wobble, the astronauts thought that a meteor had hit the lunar module *Aquarius*. To protect the command module *Odyssey*, Swigert tried to close the tunnel that connected *Aquarius* to *Odyssey*. He slammed the hatch shut and wrestled with the lock. It wouldn't catch. Lovell took over and tried to seal the hatch. The lock wouldn't budge, and the hatch stayed open.

The astronauts strapped themselves into their seats, checked the gauges on the instrument panel, and relayed what was happening to mission control in Houston. An amber warning light for the electrical system flashed. For some unknown reason, it looked as if the spacecraft had lost most of the power coming from one of two power distribution hubs. Was the reading accurate? If so, roughly half the equipment on the spacecraft would soon fail.

MISSION CONTROL

Flight controllers at mission control jumped into action. They scanned rows and rows of numbers flickering across computer screens in front of them. The headsets they wore to communicate with one another buzzed with voices reporting problems. The engineers in charge of the electrical system noted massive failures. Other teams of engineers saw failures in guidance and navigation, the system that made sure the spacecraft stayed on course. Problems also appeared in the communications network and the onboard computer. Flight controllers had never seen so many system failures on a spaceflight.

The numbers constantly changed as Apollo 13 transmitted

A group of eight astronauts and flight controllers monitor the console activity in the Mission Operations Control Room of the Mission Control Center during the Apollo 13 crisis.

data from space. But the numbers in mission control did not match the numbers on the spacecraft. On the ground, it looked as if one of the oxygen tanks in the service module was empty. On the spacecraft, the oxygen tank seemed fine. The readings on the mission control computer screens didn't make sense. Flight controllers thought there must be a glitch in the sensors that took the readings.

Flight controllers reported their findings to Gene Kranz, the flight director. He would decide what to do. The flight controllers recommended solutions to the various problems they observed and told Kranz how the issue would impact the rest of the mission. But the flight controllers' reports didn't match up. The numbers didn't form a pattern. Kranz pulled the jumble of conflicting reports together. Cool under pressure, he quickly analyzed the data and decided the trouble must be faulty instruments. It had to be. In all his years at NASA, Kranz had never seen anything like this.

HOW BAD IS BAD?

As Kranz and his team worked through the data, the radio signal from the spacecraft to mission control crackled. The main antenna that provided communication from *Odyssey* to NASA had stopped working. Without a radio link, the astronauts would be trapped in space with no way to contact Earth. Four low-power antennas took over, but data transmitted to mission control was spotty. This made it difficult for flight controllers to sort through the confusing numbers on their screens and figure out the scope of the problem. They asked the crew for the latest reading from *Odyssey*.

The astronauts scanned the instrument panel, and their spirits sank. Readings that had appeared good moments before looked dreadful. One of two oxygen tanks was empty. The other was rapidly draining away. The astronauts needed oxygen on the spacecraft to breathe. The oxygen was also needed to power the spacecraft's fuel cells.

Three fuel cells in the service module supplied electrical power to the spacecraft. Fuel cells also provided water for drinking and for cooling equipment. Two of the three fuel cells were dead. The third was dying. NASA had an unbreakable rule that to make a lunar landing, all three fuel cells had to be working. Lovell knew that if the readings were accurate, he would not be able to land on the moon.

Odyssey wobbled and lurched. In response, automatic thrusters fired in an attempt to correct the spacecraft's attitude, or orientation, in space. Lovell tried to control *Odyssey* with manual controls, but as soon as he got the spacecraft straightened out, it

Mission Control

The Mission Control Center in Houston, Texas, monitored spaceflights from liftoff through recovery. Flight controllers worked in teams so they could monitor flights in shifts around the clock. Apollo 13's flight directors chose the colors white, black, maroon, and gold to designate their teams. Within each team, engineers focused on specific aspects of the flight. One group monitored the guidance and navigation systems to make sure the spacecraft stayed on course. Other engineers were in charge of the electrical components, life-support systems, and communications networks.

The mission control room was arranged in four tiers. Flight controllers sat in front of desktop consoles with big, bulky monitors along each tier. Handles on each side of the monitor allowed service personnel to pull them out for repairs. Flight controllers found themselves gripping these handles tightly during stress. After the explosion on Apollo 13, the flight director saw many controllers clutching their "security handles."

drifted again. Frustrated, Lovell unbuckled his seat belt, floated to the window, and looked out.

What he saw made his blood run cold.

A thin, white, gassy cloud surrounded the spacecraft and extended for miles in all directions. "It looks to me," Lovell told mission control, "that we are venting something. We are venting something out . . . into space."

"Roger. We copy your venting," said mission control.

"It's a gas of some sort."

Mission control operated by a clear set of guidelines: "Crew safety is the first priority. If you don't know what to do, do nothing (you may make it worse). Readily admit that you don't know something, when you don't."

First operational in June 1965, Mission Operation Control Room 2 is most famous for its use during both the Apollo 11 moon landing and the Apollo 13 crisis. It served as flight operations/mission control for nine Gemini missions and eleven Apollo missions. It has been classed as a National Historic Landmark and has been restored to the exact condition it was in during the Apollo 11 moon landing.

PUTTING THE PIECES TOGETHER

The venting changed everything.

The astronauts in space and the flight controllers at NASA knew the problems on Apollo 13 were more than faulty instruments. The spacecraft was spewing something into space like a shaken soda can with a hole in it. They figured it must be oxygen since one oxygen tank was empty and the other was steadily decreasing. An oxygen leak also explained the power loss. Fuel cells used oxygen to generate electrical power. Nobody knew why the spacecraft was losing the precious gas. But whatever the cause, the astronauts and their broken spacecraft were in serious danger. They were closer to the moon than they were to Earth.

Landing on the moon was out. The mission then was to bring the crew home alive.

Flight controllers worked together to figure out how to help the astronauts and their dying spacecraft. But so many problems demanded attention that they didn't know where to start. "It was probably the most stressful time in my life," said flight controller Sy Liebergot. "There was a point where panic almost overcame me."

To make sure everyone began at the same place, white team director Kranz asked the crew to check the gauges, switches, and dials on the spacecraft for the latest readings. Kranz wanted to make sure the numbers they saw on the ground matched the numbers in space. "Let's everybody keep cool," Kranz told the controllers. "Let's solve the problem, team . . . let's not make it any worse by guessing."

Flight controllers sent instructions to the crew. To conserve power, the astronauts switched off nonessential equipment. They rerouted systems so mission control could trace the source of the problem. Back and forth, the men in space read gauges and took equipment readings. And the men on the ground made adjustments. "Okay, 13," mission control told the crew. "We've got lots and lots of people working on this; we'll give you some dope as soon as we have it, and you'll be the first one to know."

The astronauts on Apollo 13 and the flight controllers at mission control in Houston realized the crew needed to move into the lunar module *Aquarius* until mission control figured out how to bring the astronauts home.

A RACE AGAINST TIME

Mission control estimated that the remaining oxygen tank in the service module would be empty in less than two hours. When that happened, the last fuel cell would die and the spacecraft would lose the ability to generate electrical power, provide oxygen, and produce water. Fighting panic, they realized it would take the spacecraft about one hundred hours to make it back to Earth.

The command module had its own small oxygen tank, known as the surge tank, for the crew's air supply during the final two hours of reentry. The dying fuel cell was drawing oxygen from the surge tank to keep power flowing. The command module also had three small batteries that supplied power during reentry. One of the reentry batteries was also supplying power to the spacecraft. Since the command module was the only part of the spacecraft with a heat shield, the astronauts had to use it to get home. The first priority, then, was to save the oxygen in the surge tank and the power in the reentry batteries. Mission control directed the crew to shut down both systems.

The lunar module *Aquarius* was a separate spacecraft. It had its own power supply and life-support systems. The astronauts realized they would have to move into *Aquarius* until mission control figured out how to get them home. *Aquarius* was designed to carry two astronauts for two days. But three men would have to live in the spacecraft for four days.

By the time the astronauts and mission control decided to use *Aquarius* as a lifeboat, the crew had only fifteen minutes to get the spacecraft up and running before *Odyssey* shut down completely. The procedure normally took two hours. It was a race against time.

Lovell and Haise began powering up *Aquarius* while Swigert powered down *Odyssey*. The radio crackled as questions flew through the air to Houston and instructions zipped back up to space. As Swigert rushed through a complicated checklist, shutting down systems one switch at a time, he had to be accurate as well as fast. Since the crew would use *Odyssey* for reentry, he had to power down its systems in precisely the right order and hope that when the time came to turn them back on, they would. Lovell and Haise faced similar pressure. They had to turn on only the bare minimum life-support systems on *Aquarius* or the spacecraft would run out of breathable air, water, and power long before they reached Earth.

The astronauts also had to transfer all of *Odyssey*'s guidance and navigation data onto *Aquarius* before the power ran out. Without it, they would be lost in space, traveling in an endless loop with no way to find the correct course for home. Lovell made the calculations to convert *Odyssey*'s guidance numbers to the *Aquarius* system. But before Haise entered them into the computer, Lovell called mission control. "Houston," he said, "I want you to double-check my arithmetic." The accuracy of the figures could be the difference between life and death for the crew.

Several flight controllers did the math and confirmed Lovell's numbers. Haise entered them into the computer. The crew worked frantically to complete their *Aquarius* power-up and *Odyssey* power-down procedures accurately. The radio crackled as questions flew through the air to Houston and instructions zipped back up to space.

When Swigert shut down the last piece of equipment on *Odyssey*, the spacecraft became cold and dark. Then he floated down the tunnel to *Aquarius*.

"It's up to you now," he told Lovell and Haise.

As command module pilot, Swigert had little experience in the lunar module. He would have to rely on *Aquarius* experts Lovell and Haise to keep the strange-looking spacecraft running smoothly until it was time to turn *Odyssey* back on.

"Okay," Lovell told mission control. "*Odyssey* is completely powered down, according to the procedure that you read to Jack."

"Roger, we copy," said mission control. "That's where we want to be, Jim."

The astronauts looked around their cramped home. *Aquarius* was built for a specific task. Two men were meant to float it away from *Odyssey*, touch it down on the lunar surface, and then fly it back up to the command module after their exploration of the moon was complete. *Aquarius* would have to do much more in the days ahead. Would it be able to complete all the tasks they needed it to perform?

The crew took a breath after the hectic pace of the last few hours. NASA officials called the astronauts' families on landline telephones to tell them about the crisis in space. In 1970 there were no cell phones, websites, or social media to report news the instant it happened. People relied on newspapers, radios, and television reports to keep up with what was happening in the world. Friends and neighbors streamed to the astronauts' homes to offer support. Newspapers scrambled to write stories about the crippled spacecraft for the morning editions. Television stations broadcast special reports. ABC science editor Jules Bergman estimated the astronauts had a 10 percent chance of making it home alive.

4
LUNAR LIFEBOAT

IF THIS CREW GETS BACK, IT WILL BE BECAUSE OF THE ABSOLUTE FAITH THE CREW AND THE [FLIGHT] DIRECTORS HAVE IN EACH OTHER.

—NASA TECHNICIAN

Flight controllers, engineers, scientists, and technicians rushed to mission control when they heard about the explosion on Apollo 13. NASA called on everyone who had worked on the spacecraft to help figure out how to get the astronauts home, including Ken Mattingly, the command module pilot most familiar with the Apollo 13 spacecraft. Mattingly had been replaced from the crew because of his exposure to German measles, but he had not developed the disease. Mattingly tested procedures in simulators before instructions were relayed to the men in the spacecraft. In this way, mission control worked out problems on the ground before they sent the procedures to space.

The lunar module's role had been only to land on the moon and return to the command module in space. But it would have to drag the powered-down command module back to Earth and provide a home for three men for four days. NASA called hundreds of engineers who designed and built *Aquarius* at the Grumman Aerospace Corporation in

New York. They drove to the factory in the middle of the night through an ice storm to help bring the astronauts home.

THE BEST WAY HOME

Lovell, Swigert, and Haise were safe in *Aquarius* for the time being. They took stock of their surroundings and prepared to live in the confined space. It would be crowded and uncomfortable. There were no seats. Pilots stood to grip the controls like a captain at the helm of a ship. Swigert floated through the tunnel to *Odyssey* and grabbed food packets before they froze. He filled plastic drinking bags with water from a water gun. Some of the water splashed onto his soft cloth shoes. With the temperature in the spacecraft falling, Swigert worried his feet would freeze before his shoes dried.

As the crew gathered provisions for their new home, flight controllers decided on the safest way to get them back to Earth. Since they didn't know what caused the explosion in the service module, it was a difficult task.

Flight controllers debated two options. The first was a direct abort. In this procedure, the crew would stop the spacecraft, turn it around so it faced the opposite direction, and head straight back to Earth. A direct abort was the fastest way to bring the astronauts home. It would take about a day and a half. But nobody knew how badly damaged the powerful service module engine was. The crew would need to fire the giant engine full blast for more than five minutes. A damaged or improperly working engine could cause the spacecraft to explode, crash into the moon, or fly around in space forever.

The second option was to use *Aquarius*'s smaller engine to slingshot around the moon and use the moon's gravity to send them back toward Earth. That option would take about four days—twice as long as the direct abort procedure. Mission control worried that the astronauts would run out of power and water before they made it back to Earth.

During a lively debate in mission control, some controllers favored a direct abort, arguing that the life-support system on *Aquarius* wouldn't last long enough for the astronauts to survive a trip around the moon. Others argued for the slingshot method, citing the dead service module as proof that its engine probably

Fine Dining in Space

The food astronauts eat in space has improved over the years. Project Mercury astronauts ate semiliquid food stored in tubes. It was like eating baby food squeezed out of a toothpaste container. The menu was limited, the food unappetizing, and most of the astronauts disliked squeezing the tubes. On Gemini missions, food improved. NASA eliminated squeeze tubes and created freeze-dried, bite-sized cubes. Astronauts rehydrated the food using a water gun to inject cold water into the package. Gemini astronauts had a variety of food choices, including shrimp cocktail, chicken and vegetables, butterscotch pudding, and applesauce.

The Apollo program was the first to use hot water to rehydrate food, improving the quality and introducing a wider variety of meals. New packaging also allowed Apollo astronauts to eat certain foods, such as cereal, with a spoon.

wouldn't work. Those who participated in the discussion knew that a wrong decision could mean the death of the astronauts.

The group decided on the slingshot option. The direct abort was too risky since no one knew the condition of the service module after the explosion. By going around the moon, the moon's gravity would shoot the spacecraft toward Earth without using up valuable power the astronauts needed for reentry.

After they chose to cruise around the moon, flight controllers

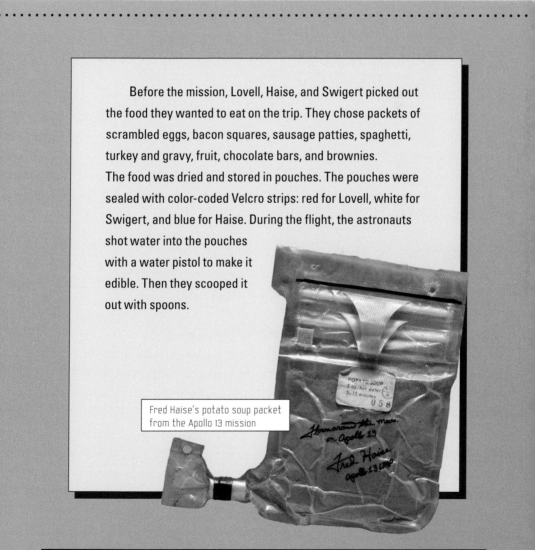

Before the mission, Lovell, Haise, and Swigert picked out the food they wanted to eat on the trip. They chose packets of scrambled eggs, bacon squares, sausage patties, spaghetti, turkey and gravy, fruit, chocolate bars, and brownies. The food was dried and stored in pouches. The pouches were sealed with color-coded Velcro strips: red for Lovell, white for Swigert, and blue for Haise. During the flight, the astronauts shot water into the pouches with a water pistol to make it edible. Then they scooped it out with spoons.

Fred Haise's potato soup packet from the Apollo 13 mission

had to change the trajectory, or path, on which the spacecraft was traveling. Apollo 13 was currently moving on a course that would land it in the Fra Mauro area of the moon. They had to change that path, or the spacecraft would whip around the moon and miss Earth by about 2,500 miles (4,023 km). Flight controllers also had to work out recovery options. Changing the path of a spacecraft changed where it landed. Would they splash down in the Pacific, Atlantic, or Indian Ocean? It was an important question because mission control had to make sure a ship was nearby to pick up the crew.

Kranz formed teams of controllers to solve key problems. One team worked on the complex calculations to set the spacecraft trajectory. Another team was in charge of making sure *Aquarius*'s power supply would last long enough to get the crew back to Earth. A third team worked on figuring out how to power up *Odyssey* for reentry when the time came. And still another team worked on a recovery plan. It was never a question of if the crew would make it home. The question was always how. Kranz told the controllers, "This crew is coming home. You have to believe it. Your people have to believe it. And we must make it happen."

GETTING ON TRACK

Mission control swiftly put together a two-part plan to put Apollo 13 on the correct track home. They told the crew they would need to burn *Aquarius*'s engine for less than a minute to get the spacecraft lined up correctly to go around the far side of the moon. The moon's gravity would whip them around and fling them toward Earth. Then the crew would perform another, longer burn to speed up the spacecraft and cut the time it would take to reach Earth. The plan was risky because each time the crew performed a burn, equipment would need to be turned on and cooled. With limited electrical power and water for cooling, it was very possible they would run out before they made it home.

Mission control wanted to do the first burn as soon as possible to conserve the limited electrical power on Aquarius. They asked the crew if they could be ready in thirty-seven minutes.

"Could you give us a little bit more time?" Lovell asked.

Preparing for a burn normally took two hours. There were precise settings to adjust, and the complicated procedure had to be exact.

Mission control stretched the time to one hour and five minutes.

To put the spacecraft on the correct path, the crew needed to make sure they started from the right attitude, or orientation, in space. To check attitude, astronauts aligned the spacecraft with stars and constellations as points of reference. But Lovell couldn't see stars because the hazy cloud of gas surrounding the

Astronaut Alan B. Shepard monitors communications between the Apollo 13 spacecraft and the Mission Control Center from a console in the Mission Operations Control Room of the center.

spacecraft obstructed his view. Sunlight reflected off the gas and debris particles from the explosion, and it all looked like stars.

Lovell tried maneuvering the combined *Aquarius-Odyssey* spacecraft away from the debris field manually. He tried turning the spacecraft so the service module cast a shadow and blocked the sun. But steering *Aquarius* was a challenge. It felt as if it was attached to a dead refrigerator. The center of gravity was completely off, and Lovell had to learn to fly all over again. Still, no matter which way Lovell steered the ship, he couldn't identify stars. They would have to execute the burn without verifying the spacecraft's attitude and hope it sent them on a path around the moon rather than plummeting into it.

Flight controllers at mission control prepared detailed instructions for the first burn. They calculated engine angles, speed, the amount of power to use, and the length of time to run the engine. They checked and rechecked the numbers because even a slight error could mean dire consequences for the men in space. *Aquarius*'s small engine was not designed to propel the combined *Aquarius-Odyssey* spacecraft. The maneuver had never been tried. No one knew if it was powerful enough to do the job.

Lovell and Haise turned on equipment in *Aquarius* to prepare for the burn. They entered the data from mission control into the spacecraft's computer. They extended four spidery legs to get them out of the engine's way. Then they fired the engine for thirty seconds. This increased their speed and put them on the correct path to the moon. The procedure worked perfectly, and everyone breathed a sigh of relief. The crew then worked with mission control to power down as much of *Aquarius* as possible. They had to conserve every bit of its water and power.

CONSERVING CONSUMABLES

As the lunar module pilot, Haise knew every inch of *Aquarius*. He'd spent hours at the Grumman factory learning about the machine from the inside out. He knew how much oxygen, electrical power, and water the spacecraft held. And he knew it wasn't enough to support the crew all the way home. Haise had to figure out ways to stretch the limited supplies. A team of flight controllers at mission control also worked on plans to conserve the life-support systems on *Aquarius*. They worked with Grumman engineers to come up with the best strategy.

According to their calculations, there was enough oxygen to keep the astronauts alive until splashdown. The problems were electrical power and water. *Aquarius* ran on battery power instead of fuel cells as *Odyssey* did. At full power, they had enough for two days. To make the power supply last four days, the crew shut down everything that wasn't essential for survival—roughly four-fifths of the systems on the spacecraft. They switched off cabin lights, heaters, gauges, some of the communications hardware, antennas, and the computer.

When the crew finished powering down *Aquarius* to the bare minimum, the spacecraft was operating the same amount of power that it takes to run a household vacuum cleaner. The air-to-ground communications link became garbled and full of static. The crew and mission control had a hard time understanding each other.

"Houston, this is *Aquarius*." Lovell shouted as they worked to improve the connection. "The comm is very, very, very noisy. Over."

"*Aquarius*, Houston. Copy that. It's noisy on our end, too," said mission control. "Stand by while we think about it."

Mission control and the crew worked on the problem. Lovell shifted the position of the spacecraft and angled antennas to point them directly at Earth. The crew changed settings on *Aquarius*. Nothing helped. The static on the line made it nearly impossible for either side to hear. As a last resort, mission control asked the crew to turn off the air-to-ground link completely for five minutes and then turn it back on. They hoped that like a computer reboot, when the system came back online, the signal would be stronger. To the relief of all, it was.

Lack of water was another huge problem for Apollo 13. The astronauts needed water to drink, and the spacecraft needed water to cool its equipment. Haise did some calculations and realized the crew would run out of water before they reached Earth. Mission control came up with the same estimate. To conserve the precious resource, the crew ate food that did not need water, such as bread cubes and peanuts. They drank only 6 ounces (177 mL) of water each day, a fraction of the normal amount for a healthy adult. They risked dehydration, which often causes fatigue, headaches, confusion, nausea, and dizziness. But stretching their water supply seemed a more pressing need. To help stave off dehydration, they also ate food that was packaged wet, such as hot dogs.

ROLLS AND SLEEP SCHEDULES

The astronauts had not slept in more than a day. Mission control, worried that the crew would make critical mistakes because they were tired, made a sleep schedule for them. But before the astronauts rested, they had to set up a passive thermal control roll. This procedure slowly rolled the spacecraft so it didn't get too hot on the part facing the sun or too cold on the part facing away from the sun. *Aquarius* did not have an automatic system for performing this task as *Odyssey* had. Lovell struggled to set up the spin manually—not easy with *Aquarius* and *Odyssey* joined at their noses. Just when Lovell thought he had the procedure set, *Aquarius* wobbled, and the spin veered away from the sun line. He eventually managed to get the spacecraft into a slow spin.

Haise was first up on the sleep schedule. He tried to rest while Lovell and Swigert monitored the spacecraft. Then they slept, and Haise kept watch over the equipment. The crew floated into *Odyssey* to sleep, which they called the bedroom. Even though the spacecraft was turned off, plenty of oxygen

A close-up view of the lunar module *Aquarius* from the *Odyssey*.

flowed through the tunnel from *Aquarius* to keep them breathing comfortably.

But it was noisy in *Odyssey*. The open hatch that provided breathable air also brought every clank, gurgle, squeak, and hiss from *Aquarius* and every crackly word spoken between the crew and mission control. And it was nearly impossible for the astronauts to turn off their minds. As tired as they were, they couldn't stop thinking about the situation they were in and imagining all sorts of possible outcomes. No one slept long or well.

HOW FAST IS FAST?

While the crew rested, teams of flight controllers worked to find the safest way to speed up their return to Earth. They calculated three different scenarios for a burn the crew would perform after they rounded the moon. A superfast burn would run the *Aquarius* engine at full power for six minutes and cut twenty-four hours off the trip. Some flight controllers liked this plan because the spacecraft would definitely splash down before they ran out of electricity and water.

However, the crew would use nearly all their fuel on this one maneuver. Nothing would be left to make a midcourse correction later. Another disadvantage to the superfast plan was that the crew would need to jettison, or detach, the service module before the burn. Some flight controllers thought this was a bad idea. The service module fit over the base of the command module and protected its heat shield from the cold of space. They didn't want to risk exposing the heat shield to possible damage because the heat shield was the only thing that protected the astronauts from burning up in Earth's atmosphere during reentry.

The second option was a little slower than the first, so the spacecraft's power and water supply would need to stretch further. However, this burn left more fuel for later midcourse corrections. This option also required jettisoning the service module.

The final option would take the longest to return home. The crew would leave the service module attached and burn *Aquarius*'s engine for four and a half minutes. They would splash down in the Pacific Ocean a full day later than option 2. Some flight controllers worried power and water on the spacecraft wouldn't last that long. Other controllers, the group working out recovery options, were nervous about this plan for another reason. Tropical Storm Helen was heading to the same spot in the southwest Pacific Ocean as the landing site.

Flight controllers, spacecraft engineers, and NASA officials debated the plans for hours. They discussed the pros and cons and the risks and benefits of each. It was the space program's "longest night," said flight director Glynn Lunney of the black team.They decided that the slowest route to Earth was the safest. NASA trusted the flight controllers working to stretch *Aquarius*'s consumables to find enough electricity and water to get the crew home. And they didn't want to lose the service module. If the heat shield was even slightly cracked from the explosion, the harsh temperatures in space could split it wide open.

With a decision made, the meeting broke up, and flight controllers went back to work.

"What do you say we quit talking about this thing," said flight director Gerald Griffin of the gold team, "and go see if we can't do it."

5

THE MOON OUT
THE WINDOW

IT IS DIFFICULT TO SAY WHAT IS IMPOSSIBLE, FOR
THE DREAM OF YESTERDAY IS THE HOPE OF TODAY
AND THE REALITY OF TOMORROW.

—ROBERT GODDARD, ROCKETRY PIONEER

Mission control flight controllers fed instructions to the Apollo 13 crew for a long engine burn that would speed up their trip to Earth. The crew would execute the burn two hours after they emerged from the far side of the moon. That meant they had to set up the procedure before they rounded the moon and lost contact with mission control. Lovell and Haise copied the instructions into their flight plan. As updates came in, they crossed out some steps and added others. They checked and rechecked each instruction.

ALIGNING BY THE SUN

Before they attempted the burn, the crew needed to verify the alignment of the spacecraft. Guidance platforms drifted over time, and even though the short burn to slingshot the spacecraft around the moon had worked perfectly, there was no guarantee the speed-up burn would be equally successful. Starting from the proper attitude was critical. With the engine blasting for more than four minutes, the spacecraft would veer dangerously off course if it started from the wrong position in space.

In Houston, astronauts worked in simulators to find a way to align the spacecraft with stars. They set up a test spacecraft to match conditions on Apollo 13. No matter which way they turned the simulator, the debris field surrounding the spacecraft blocked stars from their view. With time running out, flight controllers decided to align the spacecraft with the sun. It was a tricky maneuver. A star was a pinprick of light in a precise spot in the sky. Aligning on a few specific points of light was an accurate way to navigate and check a spacecraft's position. But the sun was not a pinprick of light. It was a huge fiery ball. The crew would have to use dark filters to protect their eyes and look for the upper-right corner of the sun.

The crew worked together on the sun check. Lovell entered the information from mission control into *Aquarius*'s computer. He pressed a button to start the procedure and watched the attitude indicators on the instrument panel. The spacecraft slowly turned. Swigert looked for the sun out a window. Haise peered through the alignment telescope. Mission control flight controllers waited in nervous silence.

For eight minutes the spacecraft rotated. Then Swigert caught a flash of the sun. Haise spotted the upper-right corner through the telescope.

"We've got it," Lovell said. "It looks like the Sun check passes."

"We understand it checks out," said mission control. "We're kind of glad to hear that."

BEHIND THE MOON

As the spacecraft approached the moon, the moon's gravity pulled it in. The closer they got, the faster they flew. At 6,000 miles (9,656 km) per hour, shadows lengthened and stars lit up the sky. Apollo 13 slipped behind the moon, and the crew lost contact with mission control for twenty-five minutes. Lovell had seen the view out the spacecraft windows when he circled the moon on Apollo 8. But it was a new experience for Haise and Swigert. They grabbed their cameras and snapped pictures out the windows. "We were . . . disappointed and sick that we could not land on the moon," said Haise. "We had lost a mission. We had worked a lot of years, and seemingly for nothing."

After they emerged from behind the moon, Lovell was anxious to prepare for the speed-up burn. But his crew was busy snapping pictures out the windows. "If we don't get home, you'll never get them developed," he reminded them.

Swigert and Haise stored the cameras, and Lovell checked in with mission control. He learned that the third stage Saturn V rocket had crashed onto the moon as planned. Equipment left behind from Apollo 12 sent data about the impact to mission

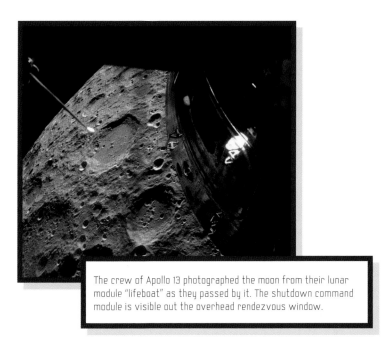

The crew of Apollo 13 photographed the moon from their lunar module "lifeboat" as they passed by it. The shutdown command module is visible out the overhead rendezvous window.

control. "Well, at least something worked on this flight," Lovell said.

A SPEED-UP BURN

The crew worked with mission control to prepare for the long burn. They knew they had to get it right if they had any hope of getting home. The astronauts turned on equipment and powered up *Aquarius* in a carefully arranged sequence. Mission control checked instrument readings from the ground and reminded the crew to stop the burn if they ran into trouble. NASA officials and reporters watched from a mission control viewing room, ready to relay the results to a waiting world.

Mission control counted down to start the procedure. The crew burned the *Aquarius* engine for four and a half minutes. The maneuver increased their speed and cut ten hours off the trip to Earth. Splashdown would be in the Pacific Ocean. NASA sent a recovery ship to the area to avoid a delay in retrieving the astronauts. They hoped Tropical Storm Helen would not be there to greet the ship.

"That was a good burn," mission control told the relieved crew. "Roger," said Lovell.

The success of the speed-up burn was a turning point in the Apollo 13 mission. Every second brought the astronauts closer to home instead of farther away from it.

After the engine burn, some flight controllers wanted the crew to turn off the equipment on *Aquarius* and get some sleep. Others insisted they set up a passive thermal control roll to distribute the sun's heat evenly before they rested. The astronauts had barely slept in two days. They were so tired that they would make costly mistakes, argued the sleep advocates. It won't matter how tired they

Old-Style Film Cameras

Smartphones and digital cameras store images electronically as digital files. You can see your pictures immediately and share them by cell phones, email, apps, and websites. In 1970, cameras stored images on film. Astronauts could not see the images until they returned to Earth and developed the exposed film through a multistep chemical process.

First, the technician washed the film in a chemical bath. This created a negative, which was hung in a dust-free room to dry. Technicians inspected the negatives for damage and created contact prints. These printed images were the same size as the negative. NASA workers used contact prints so they could wade through thousands of images and choose the best ones. They enlarged the selected images by projecting the negative onto chemically sensitized photographic paper exposed to light.

are if the spacecraft burns up or freezes, said those in favor of rolling.

Kranz decided that the crew could rest after they set up the roll. Lovell and Haise worked to set up the slow spin. But the joined *Aquarius-Odyssey* spacecraft wobbled as it did the last time they tried to set up the roll. For two hours, they struggled to get rid of the wobble. At last, they got Apollo 13 into a slow spin. Then they powered down *Aquarius*.

Haise took the first sleep cycle. Then Lovell and Swigert slept. But it was like trying to sleep inside a refrigerator. "The inside of the *Odyssey*, our bedroom, kept getting colder and colder," said Lovell. "It eventually got down pretty close to the freezing point, and it was just impossible to sleep in there." The three men huddled in *Aquarius*. Their body heat helped keep them warm in the tiny space.

POISON AIR

As the crew tried to relax, another problem popped up. *Aquarius* was filling with poison. With every breath, the crew released carbon dioxide into the air. *Aquarius* contained air scrubbers, canisters of lithium hydroxide, to purify the air. But there weren't enough filters to support three men for four days. As the hours passed, the carbon dioxide level in the spacecraft rose. If it continued unchecked, the astronauts would suffer from carbon dioxide poisoning—illness followed

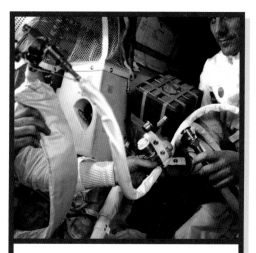

Interior view of *Aquarius* during the trouble-plagued journey back to Earth. This photograph shows some of the temporary hose connections and apparatus that were necessary when the three astronauts moved from the command module to use the lunar module as a lifeboat. In the background is a jury-rigged air filter that the astronauts built to use the command module lithium hydroxide canisters to purge carbon dioxide from the lunar module.

by falling asleep and never waking up. The astronauts needed more filters if they were going to survive.

Engineers in Houston got to work and built a filter using only materials they knew the astronauts had on the spacecraft. Once they had built a working, makeshift filter, they read the instructions to the astronauts line by line. "This contraption will look like a mailbox when you get it all put together," they said.

The astronauts gathered supplies. Swigert ripped off the cardboard cover of the flight plan. The crew grabbed duct tape, plastic bags, space suit hoses, and socks. Working together, they built the filter a step at a time. It took about an hour. Then they attached it to a wall and listened for the sound of air flowing through the device.

With his ear pressed against the canister, Swigert heard air hissing through the filter. The contraption worked. Little by little, the carbon dioxide level fell.

THE WORLD WATCHES

Before the explosion on Apollo 13, news coverage of the spaceflight was brief. Newspapers in the United States and around the world printed small articles about the mission. The flight seemed too perfect, and the public grew bored. The United States had already landed on the moon twice. It wasn't exciting anymore.

After the explosion, the whole world watched events unfold. NASA held press conferences to keep the media informed. Newspapers around the world splashed the latest updates across headlines. They increased their print runs to feed a public hungry for news. People gathered around television sets and milled in the streets discussing the damaged spacecraft. Reporters interviewed some of them for their reactions to the crisis. Although everyone wanted the astronauts to return to Earth safely, not everyone was a fan of the space program. Some people thought the cost of spaceflight was too high. They believed the money could be put toward solving the nation's many social problems.

A Great Space Hack

When we breathe, we inhale oxygen and exhale carbon dioxide (CO_2). On Earth, plants remove extra carbon dioxide from the air. But in zero gravity, a lithium hydroxide filter has to remove carbon dioxide. If astronauts breathe the carbon dioxide, they'll get sick.

Ed Smylie, a mechanical engineer at NASA, was responsible for developing and testing the life-support systems, space suits, and other equipment astronauts use in space. Smylie's team created one environmental control system for the spacecraft and another for the astronauts' space suits. Both systems used lithium hydroxide to absorb the CO_2 produced by the crew when they exhaled.

Soon after the explosion on Apollo 13, Smylie realized the crew would be in serious trouble if he didn't figure out a way to remove the excess CO_2. He and his team immediately began to work on a solution. They came up with a fix but needed to test it using the same canisters that were on the spacecraft. But Houston didn't have any canisters. So Smylie called the launch center at Cape Canaveral in Florida to see if they had any

The Apollo 13 crew built this "mailbox" to be able to use the command module lithium hydroxide canisters in the lunar module.

canisters. When a technician found the canisters, Smylie had the filters loaded onto a chartered jet and flown to Houston.

But before Smylie and his team ran the final test on their invention, Smylie made a quick trip home. He and Haise were neighbors, and their sons were good friends. Smylie brought Fred Haise Jr. to the Mission Control Center and let him watch the lithium hydroxide test. Smylie wanted to reassure the boy that his dad was going to be okay.

Radio and television stations interrupted regular programming with the latest developments. Marilyn Lovell and Mary Haise watched every television broadcast and listened to their husbands on squawk boxes loaned to them from NASA. The squawk boxes allowed them to hear all the communication between the crew and mission control.

The astronauts' homes filled with family and friends, many of them NASA employees. Reporters descended on Lovell's home and wanted to set up a broadcast tower on the front lawn for round-the-clock coverage. Marilyn Lovell refused. She told them if they had a problem with her decision, they could talk to her husband about it on Friday when he got home.

Around the world, churches and synagogues held religious services to pray for the astronauts. In Rome, Pope Paul VI prayed for the astronauts' safe return before ten thousand people. In India, thousands prayed at a religious festival. The Senate and the House of Representatives both passed resolutions asking all Americans to pray for the astronauts' safe return.

A dozen countries offered ships to help with the recovery of the astronauts after splashdown. Even the United States' rival, the Soviet Union, put aside their differences. Soviet premier Alexei Kosygin sent a message to President Nixon: "I want to inform you the Soviet Government has given orders to all citizens and members of the armed forces to use all necessary means to render assistance in the rescue of the American astronauts."

For four days, the world watched and waited. Would the astronauts make it back to Earth? Or would Lovell, Haise, and Swigert be the first astronauts to die in space?

6

A COLD, DARK JOURNEY

IF YOU MISSED THE ENTRY CORRIDOR BY A DEGREE, THAT'S A REAL BAD DAY.

—JERRY BOSTICK, NASA FLIGHT CONTROLLER

As people around the world watched and waited, Apollo 13 zoomed toward Earth. Lovell, Haise, and Swigert saw the moon shrink behind them. They crossed into Earth's sphere of influence, the point at which Earth's gravity started to pull them in. The spacecraft gained speed, and the crew thought about the huge task that lay ahead of them. Soon they would have to abandon their lunar lifeboat. Without a heat shield, *Aquarius* could not get them home. Somehow, they had to bring the cold, dead command module *Odyssey* back to life. Was that possible from deep space?

ANOTHER GLITCH

While Lovell and Swigert tried to sleep in *Odyssey*, Haise kept watch over *Aquarius*. He turned on a portable tape player and listened to the song "The Age of Aquarius." He gazed out the window for a last look at the receding moon and heard a thump from somewhere under his feet. Then a whump-shudder shook the spacecraft. Outside the window, what looked like icy snowflakes drifted past.

A master alarm sounded, and a battery light went on for battery 2.

Haise informed mission control, and flight controllers in Houston began scanning their systems for an explanation.

Aquarius had four batteries. Mission control noticed that battery 2 was lower than it should be and was still falling. Battery experts checked it out and learned that battery 2 had exploded. It was a small blast, and the battery still worked. But it wasn't producing as much electricity as it had before the explosion. Flight controllers assured the crew that batteries 1, 3, and 4 would pick up the slack for battery 2 and that it was a minor, survivable glitch.

But another glitch on top of all the previous glitches made Lovell nervous. After his nap, he pulled off the biomedical sensors glued to his chest. They were itchy, and turning them off would save precious power. Lovell knew that the next two days would be stressful. He didn't like the idea of the entire world watching his heart rate climb.

MIDCOURSE CORRECTION

Apollo 13 was veering off course. In the eighteen hours since the crew executed the long speed-up burn, the spacecraft had drifted. To the flight controllers in Houston, it looked as if something was pushing the spacecraft off its carefully designed path to Earth. *Odyssey* was turned off. Only a few pieces of equipment were turned on in *Aquarius*. Mission control didn't know what was causing the spacecraft to drift, but they knew they had to correct it.

When the spacecraft entered Earth's atmosphere, it had to be within a narrow corridor. If it came in too shallow, it would bounce off like a stone skipping across a pond and head back into space for an endless orbit. If it came in too steep, the spacecraft would burn up in the atmosphere.

Apollo 13 was coming in too shallow.

The astronauts needed to perform another burn, this time with the computer and guidance system turned off to save the remaining precious bits of power. They would have to execute the burn manually.

Mission control saw another problem developing. The pressure in *Aquarius*'s helium tank was rising. The amount of pressure was important because helium moved fuel into the combustion chamber for engine burns. A pressure-relieving burst disk was built into the gas line. When the pressure got too high, it would vent helium out to space and relieve the pressure. But when the helium vented, it could throw the spacecraft farther off course. And if the helium vented, the crew would not be able to fire the engine.

Mission control worked on a plan to perform the midcourse correction burn before the helium blowout. To align the spacecraft before the burn, the crew used an old technique from Apollo 8. Lovell remembered testing the procedure on his earlier mission. The crew pointed Apollo 13 in the right direction by using Earth's terminator, the line that separated day from night on the planet's surface, as a reference marker. While Lovell sighted on Earth, Haise looked through the alignment telescope at the sun. The two points of reference confirmed the spacecraft was positioned correctly.

The astronauts worked together to perform the fifteen-second burn. Lovell fired the engine and controlled the spacecraft's roll. Haise kept Apollo 13 oriented correctly. Swigert timed the procedure with his wristwatch. Once again, the astronauts proved they were terrific pilots. Apollo 13 was back in the center of the reentry corridor.

Three hours after the midcourse correction, the crew heard a dull pop and hiss beneath the floor of *Aquarius*. Lovell looked out the window. "I noticed a lot of sparklies going out," he told mission control. Houston confirmed what the crew suspected. The helium burst disk had ruptured. Lovell noted that when the helium vented, the spacecraft changed the direction and speed of its passive thermal control roll. He talked it over with mission control. They decided that as long as the sun's heat stayed evenly distributed by the roll, they would be able to leave it alone.

COLD, DAMP, AND YUCKY

The temperature in *Odyssey* hovered around freezing. The astronauts could see their breath. Water droplets formed on the walls, windows, and instrument panels. The combination of cold and damp chilled the astronauts. Lovell and Haise pulled on the heavy boots they would have worn on the moon to stay warm.

"Going back up into the refrigerator," said Swigert when it was time for him to rest.

"I thought it was the bedroom," said mission control.

"Well, it's got a new name now because it is about 30 degrees [17°C] cooler."

THANK YOU, KATHERINE JOHNSON

Katherine Johnson, an African American NASA mathematician, began her career at the agency performing mathematical calculations to check NASA's newly installed computers. When the Soviet Union launched *Sputnik* in 1957, she began calculating trajectories of spacecraft and satellites. She worked on Project Mercury missions, and astronaut John Glenn asked her to check the numbers by hand that the NASA computers had calculated for his spacecraft's trajectory. She did, and when the figures matched, Glenn felt confident to make his historic flight on *Friendship 7*.

After Project Mercury, Johnson joined the Space Mechanics Division at NASA where she calculated the trajectory for Apollo 11's flight to the moon. She considered her greatest contribution to the space program her work on the lunar rendezvous. Johnson fixed the precise time the lunar module needed to leave the moon's surface to meet and dock with the orbiting command module. She also computed backup navigational charts

It was so uncomfortable in the command module that Haise stretched out in the 3-foot-wide (0.9 m) tunnel between *Aquarius* and *Odyssey* and tried to sleep there. Swigert slept on the floor of *Aquarius* with a restraint wrapped around his arm to keep from floating.

Since the explosion, the astronauts had stuck to their strict intake of 6 ounces (177 mL) of water per day. As the spacecraft approached Earth, they were beginning to feel the effects of dehydration. Focusing clearly was becoming more difficult. Haise felt feverish and achy. Their food choices were limited because they ate only food that didn't need water. Some food packets were for astronauts to use during electronic failures. Mission control used Johnson's research on backup parameters and charts to position Apollo 13 for the midcourse correction burn. This exact positioning allowed the astronauts to execute the burn and put them on the correct path to Earth.

Johnson's career with NASA was portrayed in the best-selling 2016 book, *Hidden Figures* by Margot Lee Shetterly, and in an Academy Award–nominated film. A pioneer in space science, she has received awards from around the globe and continues to inspire people with her love for physics and math.

NASA space scientist and mathematician Katherine Johnson poses for a portrait at NASA's Langley Research Center in 1966 in Hampton, Virginia.

frozen. They lived on peanut cubes and sandwich spread. As the hours passed, their cozy home became far less cozy.

Normally, liquid waste was dumped out of the spacecraft through a venting system that shot it out into space. But since Apollo 13 kept drifting off course, mission control worried that venting urine would throw them farther off course. The crew had to store their liquid waste in plastic bags for the rest of the spaceflight. After a few days, bags of urine were everywhere.

SPACE SUIT OR JUMPSUIT

The astronauts thought about putting on their space suits to keep warm. Worn during liftoff, the space suits had add-ons for walking on the surface of the moon. Each suit contained a liquid-cooling garment that looked like long underwear woven with a network of fine plastic water tubes. Circulating water kept the temperature inside the suit comfortable for the astronauts. Over the cooling garment, astronauts wore a heavy-duty pressure suit. The inside layer of the multilayered pressure suit contained lightweight nylon with fabric vents. The middle layer consisted of neoprene-coated nylon to hold pressure, and the outer layer was made of nylon to restrain the pressurized layers beneath. The pressure suit felt like a scuba wet suit laced over a set of football pads.

But the crew couldn't turn on the suit's cooling system because it used too much power. Without airflow, the astronauts would sweat inside the heavy space suits. They would need to crawl out of the suits at times to cool off, and then they'd be exposed to the chilly air, soaking wet. So the crew stayed in their jumpsuits and shivered as the spacecraft limped home.

THE LAST TWENTY-FOUR HOURS

The final day of the spaceflight was the busiest for the astronauts. Mission control gave the crew a detailed checklist of all their tasks to get ready for splashdown. The checklist gave instructions for each event and the exact time the astronauts would perform the tasks.

One of the first items was to recharge *Odyssey*'s batteries using power from *Aquarius*. During reentry, the spacecraft used reentry batteries to supply all of its power. After the explosion, *Odyssey* had automatically pulled power from one of its three reentry batteries to try to keep itself alive. "We're 20 amp-hours short on one of the entry batteries, and we've got to juice that up to get you home," mission control told the crew.

The astronauts worried the lunar module didn't have power to spare. Wouldn't *Aquarius* run out of power if it gave some to *Odyssey*? Also, Lovell pointed out, the procedure reversed the electrical currents from their normal paths. The command module fed electrical power to the lunar module, not the other way around. Would reversing the flow cause a short circuit?

Mission control reassured the crew. Turning off most of the lunar module's equipment had conserved power so well that *Aquarius* had power to spare. Flight controllers explained the procedure to draw current from *Aquarius* to *Odyssey*. It had never been done or tested, but mission control felt it would work.

For three days, the crew had watched flight controllers solve problems that seemed unsolvable. They knew everyone at NASA was working as hard as they could to bring them home. And, as mission control reminded them, without a battery charge, there was no way the astronauts would make it back to Earth. The crew executed the procedure and charged one of *Odyssey*'s batteries for fifteen hours. Then they topped off another battery for about two hours.

While the batteries charged, the crew completed another task to prepare for reentry. They added weight to the command module. The calculations for reentry assumed moon rocks would be on board.

The crew transferred equipment from *Aquarius* to *Odyssey* to make up for the lack of moon rocks.

A POWER-UP PLAN

A team of engineers at mission control had been working continually to find a way to power up the command module for reentry. Normally, the power-up sequence took a full day. In a slow, precise process, technicians turned on each piece of equipment and checked it before moving on to the next. They used thousands of amp hours of ground power to warm up each system and make sure it worked properly. But the normal power-up procedure would not work on Apollo 13. Flight controllers had to find a way to bring the dead command module back to life using no more than 43 amps.

Flight controllers knew they could not turn on every system on the spacecraft. They had to figure out which systems to turn on, how much power they each would use, and the order for switching them on. They tried one configuration, then another, to come up with a plan that didn't exceed the limited resources. Each time they updated the procedure, Ken Mattingly tested it in a simulator to make sure no glitches occurred when they passed the instructions to the crew.

The spacecraft would reach Earth on Friday, regardless of whether the plan was ready. Mission control worked to find a solution before time ran out.

The crew in space grew restless. They knew that they were tired and that could cause them to make mistakes. They wanted time to study the power-up plan and make sure all three of them clearly understood each instruction.

"Just a reminder," Lovell told mission control. "It's less than twenty-four hours to go." He asked for any procedures they had, "so I can run through them with the crew and make sure we get all our signals straight."

"Roger that, Jim," said mission control. "We are trying to get the procedures finished and up to you as quickly as we can."

Finally, the checklist was ready. Since 1970 was pre-internet, mission control could not email the plan to the crew. They weren't able to upload the instructions from a powerful computer on the ground. Mattingly joined the mission control crew. He had tested the procedure in a simulator, so he read the instructions to Swigert—one line at a time.

It was slow going. Mattingly read an instruction. Swigert wrote it down using every scrap of paper he could find. Then Swigert repeated it, and mission control checked to make sure it was correct. Back and forth they went. Sometimes the communications signal dropped, and they had to repeat themselves.

It took nearly two hours for Swigert to copy the procedures. There were hundreds of intricate steps. And each one of them had to be exact. After Swigert finished the command module instructions, mission control read Haise the final checklist for the lunar module. The crew would not execute the plan for several hours. They studied it and discussed it. They made sure there were no conflicts between instructions for the command module and for the lunar module.

"If you have any questions," Mattingly said, "after you mull it over, why, we're always available. Just ask us what you're thinking about."

"Okay," said Swigert. "That's what we're going to do."

Before he signed off, Mattingly assured the crew that they had tested and retested the procedures. "We think we've got all the little surprises ironed out for you."

"I hope so," said Swigert, "because tomorrow is examination time."

7
SPLASHDOWN

ALL WE NEEDED NOW WAS A CONTINUATION OF THE EXPERTISE WE SEEMED BLESSED WITH, PLUS A LITTLE LUCK.

—JIM LOVELL

The severely damaged service module photographed by the Apollo 13 crew just after jettisoning

Apollo 13 was traveling at more than 6,000 miles (9,656 km) per hour. "I'm looking out the window now," said Lovell, "and that Earth is whistling in like a high-speed freight train."

Mission control encouraged the astronauts to get some sleep. The final hours of the spaceflight would be packed with complex procedures the crew needed to execute perfectly. Houston wanted the men to be at their best. Lovell, Haise, and Swigert tried to rest, but none of them got much sleep. Besides the frigid temperature, the crew had a lot on their minds. They knew that any one of a thousand things could go wrong during reentry. Would this be the last night of the spaceflight or their last night?

Swigert could not stop thinking about the huge responsibility that rested on his shoulders. As command module pilot, the majority of the work would be his. He saw himself pressing the wrong button by mistake. Instead of releasing the service module, in Swigert's nightmare, he released the lunar module with Lovell and Haise inside. Finally, Swigert gave up trying to sleep. He found a piece of paper, tore off a corner, and wrote *NO* on it. Then he floated up to *Odyssey* and taped it over the lunar module jettison switch.

THE LAST SIX HOURS

Mission control checked the power usage numbers on *Aquarius*. The spacecraft had more power than expected at this time in the flight, even after charging *Odyssey*'s batteries. "We figured out a way for you to keep warm," they told Lovell. "We decided to start powering you up now."

"Sounds good," said Lovell. "You're sure we have plenty of electrical power to do this?"

"That's affirmative. We've got plenty of power to do it."

Lovell and Haise worked together to power up *Aquarius*. Almost immediately, the temperature in the spacecraft started to rise. It felt wonderful to the weary travelers.

After the crew began the *Aquarius* power-up, mission control informed them that the spacecraft was shallowing out again. If they didn't correct it, Apollo 13 would enter the atmosphere at the wrong angle and miss Earth completely. The crew needed to do another midcourse correction burn to get them back on the right track.

Writing the procedure for the burn was not easy. Mission control didn't know what was causing Apollo 13 to drift off course. They couldn't predict if or how much the spacecraft would drift after the burn. Flight controllers needed to place the spacecraft in the center of the reentry corridor. They hoped it would stay there until splashdown.

Lovell and Haise checked the spacecraft's alignment with the sun and moon. Then the astronauts performed a twenty-two-second burn to correct the angle of entry. Because they could not turn on the *Aquarius* engine after the helium burst disk ruptured, they used the spacecraft's thrusters to execute the burn. That put them back in the center of the reentry corridor. After the burn, the crew maneuvered the spacecraft into the correct position to release the service module.

GETTING RID OF THE SERVICE MODULE

Swigert floated into the command module *Odyssey*. Water dripped from the windows, walls, and instrument panels. He wiped them off as well as he could. Lovell and Haise stayed in the lunar module *Aquarius*. Lovell fired *Aquarius*'s thrusters to push the *Aquarius-Odyssey* stack forward. Then Swigert triggered the explosive bolts that held the command and service modules together. When the modules separated, Lovell fired the *Aquarius* thrusters again in the opposite direction. Still connected, the lunar module and the command module backed up. The service module drifted away.

The damaged service module, photographed by the Apollo 13 crew after separation, shows an entire panel was missing.

Lovell twisted the spacecraft around so the crew could photograph the service module through their windows. The astronauts hoped the pictures would help NASA figure out what happened to their spacecraft.

The service module floated into view. The crew snapped pictures. The massive damage shocked them.

"There's one whole side of that spacecraft missing," Lovell told mission control.

"Is that right?"

"Right by the high gain antenna, the whole panel is blown out, almost from the base to the engine."

"Man, that's unbelievable!" Haise added.

Whatever happened four days ago was so violent it ripped off one whole side of the spacecraft. Wires and debris dangled out of a gaping hole. Where oxygen tank 2 was supposed to be, there was nothing but a charred cavity.

The astronauts thought about the heat shield, which covered the base of the command module. It sat against the service module, now a mangled mess, when the service module blew apart. If the heat shield was cracked or damaged in any way, the men would burn up during reentry. No fix from mission control could repair a broken heat shield zooming toward Earth. So the astronauts kept their worries to themselves. Swigert floated back down to *Aquarius*, and the crew continued preparing for splashdown.

POWERING UP *ODYSSEY*

As the command module pilot, Swigert had been mostly a bystander in the lunar module. But with Apollo 13 approaching Earth, his role in the spaceflight became critical. *Aquarius* had performed beautifully, much better than expected. But *Aquarius* couldn't get them home. Only *Odyssey* could do that, and *Odyssey* was Swigert's responsibility.

A GIANT BILL

The lunar module *Aquarius* hauled the command module *Odyssey* from the moon to Earth. Engineers at Grumman Aerospace Corporation, builder of *Aquarius*, were proud of their spacecraft's performance. The company sent a bill to North American Rockwell, builder of *Odyssey*. The bill listed charges for towing, battery charging, oxygen, and sleeping accommodations. The total came to $312,421.24. The fake invoice appeared in the *New York Times*. Grumman found it extremely amusing. North American Rockwell joked back, issuing a statement that they had not received payment for ferrying lunar modules on previous trips to the moon.

The astronauts feared the moisture in the command module had damaged the electrical systems in the spacecraft. When Swigert pushed buttons and turned switches, would the equipment short-circuit? Would it explode? Or would it simply refuse to start like a dead car battery? No one at mission control could guarantee the power-up plan would work on the cold, damp equipment. The procedure had never been done in space.

Three and a half hours before splashdown, Swigert floated through the tunnel to *Odyssey*. He carried the detailed power-up plan he had copied from mission control. Haise went with him to help bring the dead spacecraft to life. Swigert turned on heaters to warm up equipment slowly. He switched on the reentry batteries. Then he pushed buttons, flipped one switch, then the next, and so on. He worked on aligning the guidance platform, one of the most critical steps in the power-up procedure. The guidance system made sure the spacecraft stayed within the narrow reentry corridor.

Swigert loaded the alignment from the lunar module's guidance platform. But to make sure it was accurate for the command module's current position, he needed to verify it with a precise navigational fix. Mission control sent up coordinates for positioning the spacecraft with guide stars. Looking through *Odyssey*'s scanning telescope, Swigert searched for the stars. But sunlight reflected off a blizzard of white ice nuggets that had formed from *Aquarius*'s instrument cooling system, and Swigert couldn't see the stars.

Mission control sent coordinates for a guide star on the side of the spacecraft facing away from the sun. Swigert turned off a light in *Odyssey* to make it easier to see. With the light off and the spacecraft's shadow blocking the sun's glare, Swigert found the guide star and verified the spacecraft's guidance platform.

"I did a star check," he told mission control, "and it passes. It puts that star right in the telescope."

"Good enough," said mission control. "You can press on in the checklist."

As Swigert proceeded with the power-up, flight controllers in Houston waited nervously for the equipment readings to filter down to them from space. The plan called for *Odyssey* to use 43 amps of power. Any more than that and the spacecraft would run out of electricity before it reached Earth. Numbers began flickering on the screens at mission control—45 amps. They were over the limit by 2 amps.

Flight controllers scrambled to find the piece of equipment that was on when it shouldn't be. In a few minutes, they found it, radioed up to Swigert, and told him to shut it off. The total amp reading dropped to 43, and the flight controllers started breathing again.

GOODBYE, *AQUARIUS*; HELLO, EARTH

One hour before splashdown, it was time to release the lunar module. Lovell floated through the tunnel that connected *Aquarius* to *Odyssey*. He closed and sealed the hatch. Unlike Monday night, it snapped into place without a problem. Lovell then swam to his seat in the command module beside Swigert and Haise.

Swigert ripped his *NO* note off the Jettison switch on the instrument panel and crushed it in his fist. Then he flipped a switch and fired the explosive bolts that held *Aquarius* to *Odyssey*. *Aquarius* drifted away.

"Farewell, *Aquarius*," said mission control, "and we thank you."

Odyssey sped toward Earth at 25,000 miles (40,234 km) per hour. The astronauts had completed the reentry checklist from mission control. They had to wait and hope that the spacecraft was still within the narrow reentry corridor, that the heat shield would protect them from the fiery atmosphere, and that the parachutes would open to plunk them gently into the ocean. If the astronauts were afraid, they didn't show it. They knew and accepted the risks that came with spaceflight.

As Apollo 13's splashdown grew closer, friends, neighbors, and NASA employees joined the astronauts' families to watch the final moments of the mission. A driver from her nursing home drove

Marilyn Lovell (*in striped dress*), astronaut Jim Lovell's wife, watches the Apollo 13 splashdown on television with her children and friends at her home in Houston, Texas, on April 17, 1970.

Lovell's mother, Blanche Lovell, to the Lovell home. Lovell's wife, Marilyn Lovell, set up a television for his mother to watch his return to Earth. Apollo 11 astronauts Neil Armstrong and Buzz Aldrin joined her. The viewing room for mission control filled with NASA officials, politicians, astronauts, and the media. The sign on the marquee of the hotel at the front gate of the Manned Spacecraft Center expressed the thoughts of many. "Our hearts are with the Apollo 13 crew."

Everyone, it seemed, wanted to watch the end of the extraordinary journey of Apollo 13.

The three national television networks prepared to broadcast the splashdown live. In New York City, thousands watched on a giant television screen in Grand Central Station. All around the world, from England to Japan, people stopped what they were doing and rushed home to watch TV. The European Broadcasting Union called it the biggest television audience of all time.

The recovery ship, USS *Iwo Jima*, headed to the recovery site to pick up the crew. A television camera mounted on a helicopter

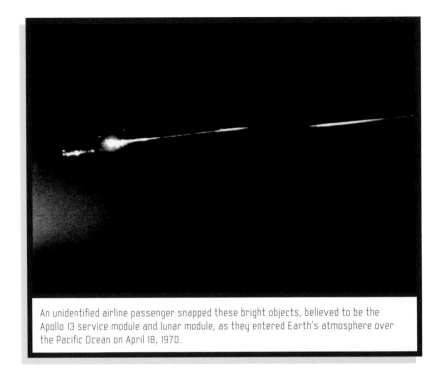

An unidentified airline passenger snapped these bright objects, believed to be the Apollo 13 service module and lunar module, as they entered Earth's atmosphere over the Pacific Ocean on April 18, 1970.

aboard the ship relayed close-up pictures of the recovery to a waiting world. The weather in the South Pacific was mild, the sea calm. The entry angle provided by flight controllers had avoided Tropical Storm Helen, and it posed no threat to the recovery efforts.

When Apollo 13 reached the upper layer of Earth's atmosphere, the astronauts would lose communication with the ground for about four minutes. Just minutes before the blackout, Swigert called mission control. "I know all of us here want to thank all you guys down there for the very fine job you did."

"That's affirm," added Lovell.

Soon after, all was silent, in the spacecraft and in mission control.

Apollo 13 plunged through the atmosphere. Friction around the spacecraft generated temperatures of 5,000°F (2,760°C) and washed over the heat shield. Flight controllers calculated the blackout to end after three minutes and twenty-three seconds. Until then, the astronauts would be in the center of a fireball. And mission control could only wait and see whether they survived reentry.

Minutes seemed like hours to mission control. No one spoke. No one moved. Flight controllers watched the clock on the wall. Three minutes passed and then three minutes and thirty seconds. When the clock reached four minutes, flight controller Joe Kerwin waited for confirmation that communications were online again before radioing the spacecraft. Silence. He waited fifteen more seconds. Still no confirmation. Finally, a signal was confirmed.

"*Odyssey*, Houston standing by. Over," said Kerwin. The spacecraft remained silent for three more seconds.

Then static on the communications loop crackled, and Swigert's voice broke through. "Okay, Joe."

Relief flooded mission control.

Apollo 13 flight directors celebrate the successful splashdown and recovery of the Apollo 13 crew. *From left*: Gerry Griffin (*giving thumbs up*), Gene Kranz, and Glynn Lunney

"Okay," said Kerwin in the calm voice of a flight controller. "We read you, Jack."

The heat shield had done its job. Only one critical task remained, and the Apollo 13 astronauts would be home. If the parachutes opened, the spacecraft would glide gently into the ocean. If they didn't open, the spacecraft would crash and the impact would crush the astronauts.

Sailors on the deck of the *Iwo Jima* scanned the partly cloudy sky. One of them shouted, and a camera operator on board the ship turned in his direction. Three red-and-white parachutes attached to the command module floated through the clouds. The image flashed across the huge screen at the front of mission control and onto television screens around the world.

Apollo 13 splashes down in the Pacific Ocean 142 hours, 54 minutes, and 44 seconds from liftoff.

THE WORLD REJOICES

A cheer went up from the deck of the recovery ship. Flight controllers at mission control stood and applauded, many with tears running down their cheeks. Mattingly relaxed for the first time in a week. The sign outside the gate of the Manned Spacecraft Center was changed to "Sigh of relief party here tonight."

Marilyn Lovell and Mary Haise laughed, cried, and hugged their children. Swigert's parents called it the best day of their lives. "It was a wonderful beginning and a beautiful landing," said his father, Dr. Leonard Swigert, "but I wouldn't give you two hoots for the interim."

WHAT-IF GAMES

Flight controllers at mission control got little sleep during the Apollo 13 crisis. Many of them stayed long after their shift ended and came in hours before their next shift began. Kranz claimed a corner of the mission control viewing room for naps. After snatching thirty to forty-five minutes of sleep, he returned to his team, ready to handle the next crisis.

Kranz and his team spent most of their time huddled in a room on the second floor of the Mission Control Center while the other three flight control teams monitored the consoles. Kranz's team shared ideas and brainstormed, hashing out the details of the plan to bring the astronauts home. The room was crowded and noisy. Controllers, engineers, and technicians filled

The Mission Operations Control Room at the Manned Spacecraft Center in Houston, Texas, during the Apollo 13 mission. Gene Kranz is pictured on the right with his back to the camera.

every chair around a long, gray table and sat cross-legged on the floor with papers, diagrams, and notes strewn around them.

The final hours of the spaceflight were the most stressful. Several flight controllers worked all night playing what-if games. *What-if games* was the term they used for thinking about possible problems that might occur and figuring out how to fix them in advance.

In Washington, DC, Nixon watched the Apollo 13 splashdown from the White House. When the astronauts landed safely, he applauded and lit a victory cigar. "There is no question in my mind that for me, personally, this is the most exciting, the most meaningful day that I have ever experienced," he said. Nixon called the astronauts' families to invite them to join him on Air Force One the following day. He planned to meet the astronauts in Hawaii and welcome the crew home.

For a few minutes, people around the world forgot their differences and celebrated the astronauts' safe return. Church bells rang. Folks clapped and cheered. Some sobbed. Others offered prayers of thanksgiving. In New York City, people poured buckets of confetti out skyscraper windows. The landing seemed nothing short of miraculous.

While celebrations rang out around the world, the helicopter from the *Iwo Jima* hovered above Apollo 13 as it bobbed in the

Commander Jim Lovell waits in a life raft in front of the command module *Odyssey* while command module pilot Jack Swigert is plucked out of the ocean and onto a waiting helicopter.

water. Recovery swimmers jumped into the water and swam to the spacecraft. They inflated a raft for the astronauts and positioned it beside the spacecraft. When the astronauts opened the hatch, a blast of cold air washed over the rescue swimmers. Haise was the first to emerge from the spacecraft. He tumbled into the raft, and the helicopter hoisted him up in a contraption that looked like a huge birdcage. Swigert was next, followed by Lovell. The recovery was flawless. In a few minutes, the astronauts stepped off the helicopter and onto the deck of the *Iwo Jima*. Waving to the ship's crew, they soaked up the warmth of the sun.

The ship's band played "Age of Aquarius," and there was a short welcome home ceremony. A Protestant chaplain offered a prayer of thanksgiving for Apollo 13's safe return. The astronauts smiled and posed for pictures. Their four-day fight for survival was over. It was almost too much to take in. Against incredible odds, they had survived.

8

WHEW, WHAT A MISSION!

THERE HAS NEVER BEEN A HAPPIER MOMENT IN THE UNITED STATES SPACE PROGRAM. ALTHOUGH THE APOLLO 13 MISSION MUST BE RECORDED AS A FAILURE, THERE HAS NEVER BEEN A MORE PRIDEFUL MOMENT.

—THOMAS PAINE, NASA ADMINISTRATOR

After the short welcome home ceremony on the *Iwo Jima*, the astronauts were whisked away to a medical facility on board the ship. A team of nine doctors examined the men for three hours. Lovell had lost 14 pounds (6.4 kg). Swigert and Haise lost between 5 and 10 pounds (2.3 and 4.5 kg) each. All three men were dehydrated. Haise also had a fever and an infection. Dr. Keith Baird described it as a minor problem. He stated that the men were tired but in good health.

The married astronauts, Lovell and Haise, called their wives. Swigert called his parents. The men ate a hearty meal and slept. The next morning, a helicopter flew the crew from the *Iwo Jima* to Pago Pago, American Samoa, an American territory in the South Pacific. Thousands of colorfully dressed locals greeted the astronauts at the airport. The crew soaked up the warmth of sun-drenched green hills covered with exotic flowers. They watched a performance of Samoan songs and dances. Then they flew to Honolulu, Hawaii, in an air force jet to meet the president.

HOMECOMING CELEBRATIONS

Nixon flew to Houston the day after the astronauts landed. Under cloudy skies, he stood on a raised wooden platform in front of the Manned Spacecraft Center at NASA. Behind him loomed a towering full-scale model of a lunar module. A band played military songs. Nixon presented the Presidential Medal of Freedom to the Apollo 13 Mission Operations Team. "The three astronauts did not reach the Moon, but they reached the hearts of millions of people in America and in the world," Nixon said. "We often speak of scientific miracles, forgetting that these are not miraculous happenings at all, but rather the product of hard work, long hours,

Rear Admiral Donald C. Davis, commanding officer of Task Force 130, the Pacific Recovery Force for manned spacecraft missions, welcomes the Apollo 13 crew members aboard the USS Iwo Jima.

and disciplined intelligence. The men and women of the Apollo 13 mission operations team performed such a miracle, transforming potential tragedy into one of the most dramatic rescues of all time." Sigurd Sjoberg, director of flight operations, accepted the award for the team.

After the ceremony in Houston, Nixon and the astronauts' families flew on Air Force One to Honolulu, Hawaii. Lovell, Haise, and Swigert met them there. When the astronauts stepped off the silver air force jet from Samoa, their families threw their arms around them. President Nixon and First Lady Pat Nixon stood smiling nearby.

Thousands cheered as Nixon welcomed the crew home. "Your mission served the cause of international understanding and goodwill," Nixon said. "Never before in the history of man

PRESIDENTIAL MEDAL OF FREEDOM

The Presidential Medal of Freedom is the United States' highest civilian honor. President Harry Truman began the award as a way to recognize civilians during World War II. President John F. Kennedy expanded the scope of the award to include cultural achievements. The president of the United States picks people who have made an important contribution to the United States. Winners include writers Maya Angelou, Toni Morrison, and Harper Lee; athletes Tiger Woods, Billie Jean King, and Willie Mays; musicians Elvis Presley, Stevie Wonder, and Diana Ross; actors Tom Hanks, Sidney Poitier, and Meryl Streep; philanthropists Oprah Winfrey and Bill and Melinda Gates; scientist Stephen Hawking; and mathematician Katherine Johnson.

President Richard M. Nixon stands with the Apollo 13 crew after presenting them the Presidential Medal of Freedom at the ceremony at Hickam Air Force Base, Hawaii.

have more people watched together, prayed together, and rejoiced together at your safe return, than on this occasion."

Nixon read the citation engraved on the astronauts' medals. "Adversity brings out the character of a man. Confronted suddenly and unexpectedly with grave peril in the far reaches of space, he demonstrated a calm courage and quiet heroism that stand as an example to men everywhere. His safe return is a triumph of the human spirit—of those special qualities of man himself we rely on when machines fail, and that we rely on also for those things that machines cannot do." Then Nixon hung the Medal of Freedom around each of the astronauts' necks.

The Apollo 13 crew spent a day in the sun, relaxing with their families in Hawaii. Then they flew to Houston on Air Force Two, the backup presidential plane. Floodlights lit a brief ceremony at Ellington Air Force Base, where thousands of NASA employees welcomed the crew home. A band played "Age of Aquarius," and a banner that read "Whew, What a Mission!" fluttered in the breeze.

Lovell spoke first. "There were times when we didn't really think we would make it back here," he said. "I must admit that the only reason we are here is because of the people right out here now."

An emotional Swigert added, "Of all the welcomes home we've had, this one means the most because it was these people here that made it possible for me to be here."

The next morning, the Apollo 13 crew began mission debriefing and helping NASA figure out what went wrong with the spacecraft. NASA set up a press conference, and the astronauts described key milestones in the mission. They answered questions from the media and expressed admiration for the tireless work of mission control. "I'm very much disappointed," Lovell said, "just as Fred is and Jack, that we couldn't complete the mission. We certainly wanted to make a lunar landing. "Then he added, "Perhaps what we got out of this flight was also well worth it." A reporter asked if Lovell would fly future missions. The astronaut assured him that if NASA assigned him another spaceflight, he'd be willing to go.

Haise added that he had worked for NASA for fifteen years and planned to continue working there for another thirty. "So, I'll just do whatever job the agency decides is the best place I can be and can contribute the most."

THE INVESTIGATION

NASA had not tried to figure out what caused the explosion on Apollo 13 while the astronauts were in space. Mission control had focused all their energy on bringing the crew safely back to Earth.

Now that the astronauts had returned, Thomas Paine, NASA director, formed a commission to investigate what went wrong on the spacecraft. NASA announced that future trips to the moon would wait until the Apollo 13 investigation was complete. The agency would figure out the problem or problems, fix them, and make sure a similar crisis never occurred.

Edgar Cortright, director of NASA's Langley Research Center in Hampton, Virginia, headed the commission. Its fourteen members included Apollo 11 astronaut Neil Armstrong, engineers and administrators from NASA, and an independent observer from outside NASA. From pictures of the service module the crew brought back to Earth, the committee knew that a meteor hadn't hit the spacecraft. The blast came from within the service module. Their job focused on finding out where, how, and why.

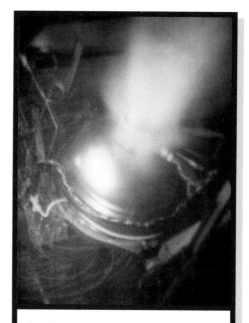

This photograph from a motion picture sequence taken during a propagation test during the postflight investigation for Apollo 13 shows the failure of the oxygen tank conduit with abrupt loss of oxygen pressure.

The committee examined the manufacturing history of the equipment in the service module. They looked at test results on the oxygen and hydrogen tanks and noted problems that had developed during installation and testing. Before long, they isolated several problems with oxygen tank no. 2. NASA engineers ran laboratory tests to verify their findings.

After a two-month investigation, the committee concluded that a combination of mistakes caused the explosion in space. Oxygen tank no. 2 had been dropped about 2 inches (5 cm) before the flight. Technicians had examined the tank for damage and tested it to make sure it worked properly. No damage was detected, so they left the tank in place inside the service module.

During prelaunch tests at the Kennedy Space Center, the oxygen in tank no. 2 would not drain. Workers turned on heaters in the tank to boil off the oxygen. But there was a problem. The Apollo 13 spacecraft operated on 28 volts of electricity. The ground equipment at Kennedy Space Center that supplied power to the heaters worked at 65 volts. The company that made the heaters pointed out that the thermostatic switches on the heaters should also be changed to 65 volts, but engineers failed to make the change and nobody caught the mistake. The switches continued to operate at 28 volts on heaters operating at 65 volts.

Apollo 14 launched from Kennedy Space Center, Florida, on January 31, 1971, at 4:03:02 p.m.

When workers drained oxygen tank no. 2, the heaters were kept on for eight hours. Normally, the temperature in the tank did not rise higher than 80°F (27°C). However, because of the voltage discrepancy, the temperature inside tank no. 2 rose to nearly 1,000°F (538°C). The high temperature melted the Teflon coating the wires inside the tank. Nobody could see that inside tank no. 2, the wires were bare and exposed. During the Apollo 13 spaceflight, when Swigert flipped the switch to turn on the heaters and stir the oxygen tank, a spark from the exposed wires started a fire, and tank no. 2 exploded.

Investigators also learned why the Apollo 13 spacecraft kept drifting off course on its trip back to Earth. Wisps of steam released from Aquarius's cooling system pushed the spacecraft off its trajectory bit by bit. Since a lunar module had never been flown back to Earth, engineers had not encountered the problem before the Apollo 13 mission.

The committee summarized its findings in a report. "The accident is judged to have been nearly catastrophic," the report stated. "Only outstanding performance on the part of the crew, mission control, and other members of the team which supported the operations successfully returned the crew to Earth."

The investigation led NASA to make several changes to Apollo spacecraft. They added a third oxygen tank and placed it in a separate area of the service module. They removed thermostat switches. They improved wire coating. They added a battery powerful enough to bring astronauts back to Earth from any point in a lunar mission. They added water storage bags to give astronauts a way to store drinking water in the command module. NASA also modified procedures to ensure Apollo 13 oversights would not happen again.

After NASA finished Apollo's spacecraft repairs, the agency was ready to continue its exploration of the moon. NASA had plans for Apollo 14 through Apollo 20. Each mission would build on the one before and include more extensive scientific experiments. But the 1970s was a difficult time for America. The Vietnam War intensified. Protests against the war increased. Many people did not support the space program any longer because of the many problems on Earth that needed solving. Congress cut NASA's budget, so NASA canceled the final three Apollo missions. The news disappointed the nine astronauts scheduled for those flights, especially Fred Haise, commander of the grounded Apollo 19 flight.

FRA MAURO ONCE MORE

Apollo 14 blasted off on January 31, 1971, nine months after Apollo 13 landed. The crew—Alan Shepard, Stuart Roosa, and Edgar Mitchell—took over the scientific mission objectives of Apollo 13 with a new and improved service module. Mechanical difficulties in the docking system almost ended the mission shortly after it began. It took six attempts for the crew to dock the command module with the lunar module. After that, the astronauts enjoyed a smooth, glitch-free ride to the moon. Then another problem developed and almost canceled the moon landing.

As Shepard and Mitchell prepared to land in the Fra Mauro region, flight controllers at mission control noticed that the spacecraft computer had received an abort command. If this command appeared when the astronauts were hovering over the lunar surface, it would end the mission. But the signal came on randomly. When Mitchell tapped on the instrument panel, it disappeared. Mission control studied their equipment readings. All systems looked good for a lunar landing. They worked with computer programmers at the Massachusetts Institute of Technology (MIT) and came up with a fix. The programmers wrote a software patch to tell the lunar module computer to ignore the abort signal. The crew in space entered the lines of code into their computer. It worked, and the astronauts proceeded with the landing.

They faced one more challenge. As the astronauts descended,

DETERMINED TO FLY

Alan Shepard (*right*), one of the seven original Mercury astronauts, was the first American to fly into space. After his journey on *Freedom 7*, Shepard was grounded from future spaceflights because of an inner ear disorder. Determined to fly again, he had surgery to drain inner ear fluid into his spinal cord. The surgery restored his equilibrium, or balance, and cleared him for spaceflight.

landing radar was supposed to bounce off the surface of the moon and tell them their altitude. But the radar didn't come on. Mission control rules were clear. If the radar wasn't working when the spacecraft reached 10,000 feet (3,048 m), they had to abort the mission. It was better to cancel than risk crashing into the moon. Haise was communicating with the crew from mission control. Haise told the crew to turn the landing radar switch off and then turn it back on. Shepard flipped the switch. Warning lights disappeared, and radar data appeared on the screen. The astronauts landed on the Fra Mauro highlands.

Command module pilot Roosa orbited the moon and took pictures of the lunar surface. Shepard and Mitchell made two four-hour moonwalks. They collected rock samples and set up experiments. They pulled a two-wheeled cart, a lunar rickshaw, to carry their equipment and samples. Shepard conducted one last experiment before he left the lunar surface. He stuck a golf club head onto a geology tool. Then he dropped a golf ball in the lunar dust and swung away. The ball was hard to hit wearing a bulky space suit. But he connected on his third swing and watched the ball sail away, traveling for close to a mile. Then Shepard and Mitchell returned to the lunar module. They lifted off from the moon, docked with Roosa in the command module, and returned to Earth.

MOON GERMS

Since the Apollo crews were the first people to return from the moon, scientists were concerned that astronauts might bring back germs that could harm life on Earth. There could be hibernating microorganisms hiding in the lunar soil samples, on the crew, or in their equipment. Crews from Apollo 11, Apollo 12, and Apollo 14 were quarantined, or placed in isolation, after splashdown. The astronauts and the material they brought back to Earth stayed in the Lunar Receiving Laboratory for twenty-one days. Medical experts agreed that an infection would display symptoms within that period. None of the astronauts showed symptoms of infection or disease. NASA scientists studied lunar soil samples under microscopes and found no sign of living organisms. The agency dropped the quarantine program after Apollo 14.

After a spacecraft returned from a lunar landing, NASA sent rock and soil samples from the moon to the Lunar Receiving Laboratory at the Manned Spacecraft Center in Houston. Scientists studied and tested the samples. They shipped some of the material to laboratories around the world for analysis. This sharing of scientific knowledge began a new era of international cooperation in space science.

The first three times Apollo astronauts landed on the moon, they were motivated by a race. NASA focused on the technology and science required to get them there and back safely. The distance astronauts could walk from their spacecraft limited their exploration. Apollo 11, Apollo 12, and Apollo 14 proved NASA had mastered the technical challenges of the journey.

The final three Apollo missions were not motivated by a race. The race had been won. The promise of scientific exploration motivated them. Apollo 15, Apollo 16, and Apollo 17 were voyages of discovery, expeditions to map another world.

9

THE LAST MEN ON THE MOON

THIS IS WHAT ALL ASTRONAUT-EXPLORERS ARE TRAINED TO DO: JOURNEY TO PERILOUS PLACES ON DANGEROUS MISSIONS—SOMETIMES MEETING THE UNEXPECTED—AND RETURN, ALIVE, WITH NEW TRUTHS, NEW KNOWLEDGE, AND NEW POSTFLIGHT WISDOM ON HOW TO MAKE FUTURE FLIGHTS SAFER AND BETTER.

—FRANCIS FRENCH AND COLIN BURGESS, *INTO THAT SILENT SEA*

Astronaut Dave Scott on the rim of Hadley Rille with the lunar rover.

Each of the final three Apollo missions sent astronauts to a different area of the moon. NASA worked with geologists to pick landing sites that offered diverse landscapes with interesting features. They set up increasingly complex experiments so the trips would provide insights into how the moon was formed. The astronauts for these missions spent months ahead of time studying geology. They worked with experts and took field trips to the Rio Grande Gorge in New Mexico and the mountains of California. They learned to identify and describe various types of geologic structures.

Lunar exploration missions needed more geology equipment than early Apollo missions. NASA upgraded the lunar module to carry the extra weight. Engineers added powerful batteries so the spacecraft could stay on the moon longer. Early lunar landings included two moonwalks of about four hours each. Lunar exploration missions included three long excursions of about seven hours each. Engineers extended the astronauts' exploration time by increasing life-support systems in the backpacks the men wore outside the spacecraft.

APOLLO 15—HADLEY RILLE

Apollo 15 launched on July 26, 1971. It was the first mission designed to investigate the moon from orbit as well as from the lunar surface. Alfred Worden, the command module pilot, operated a scientific observation platform while he orbited the moon. He conducted experiments and photographed never-before-seen images of the moon's surface. Scientists chose a mountainous region called Hadley Rille for Apollo 15's landing site. A deep channel that looked like an empty riverbed wove across the area. The mountainous terrain made the approach tricky, but David Scott and James Irwin executed the landing perfectly.

Scott and Irwin stayed on the moon for three days. On the first day, Scott hopped down the ladder from the lunar module. He looked around at the stark landscape. "As I stand out here in the wonders of the unknown at Hadley, I sort of realize there's a fundamental truth to our nature," he said. "Man must explore. And this is exploration at its greatest."

The astronauts loaded the rover, a battery-powered car with wire mesh wheels. Filled with geology equipment, cameras, and gear, the rover allowed the astronauts to roam miles from their landing site. The rover had a television camera mounted to the front. The camera allowed mission control and the world to watch the astronaut-explorers as they gathered clues to unlock the moon's mysteries.

THE LUNAR ROVER

The lunar rover was an engineering marvel. It could withstand temperature changes of more than 500°F (280°C) between lunar sun and lunar shadow. It was battery-powered and carried a communication station powerful enough to transmit to and receive from Earth. It was sturdy enough to carry equipment, cargo, and television cameras. It also contained a navigation system so the astronauts wouldn't get lost on the moon. The rover folded in on itself and was stored inside the lunar module for the trip to the moon. Astronauts tugged on lanyards, or a line, to lower the rover to the lunar surface like a drawbridge. It unfolded as it reached the ground.

Apollo 15 astronaut David Scott waits in the lunar roving vehicle for astronaut James Irwin for the return trip to the lunar module, Falcon, with rocks and soil collected near Hadley Rille. Powered by battery, the lightweight electric car greatly increased the astronauts' mobility and productivity on the lunar surface. It could carry two suited astronauts, their gear and cameras, and several hundred pounds of bagged samples.

Scott enjoyed driving his new car around the moon like a dune buggy on a lonely desert. "This is a super way to travel," he said as he zipped across the lunar dust. "This is great." The astronauts dodged craters and bounced past towering mountains. They chipped off samples of rocks, scooped dirt from various locations, and stored them in bags. They photographed all kinds of geological formations. They also set up scientific experiments on the lunar surface.

After nearly seven hours of exploring, Scott and Irwin returned to Hadley Base where the lunar module sat waiting for their return. They climbed up the ladder and took off their space suits. They ate and slept. The next morning, they prepared for their longest day of exploration.

GENESIS AND GALILEO

Scott and Irwin drove to Mount Hadley Delta. They trekked across the side of the mountain, took samples, and described the terrain for the team of geologists watching in mission control. Then they headed to Spur crater. The astronauts noticed a small white rock. It stood out against the gray dust of the moon and caught their attention. Scott lifted the rock, about the size of his fist, and examined it. Large, white crystals sparkled in the sun. Both men marveled at their find. Laboratory tests would later reveal that the stone was a piece of the moon's original crust. Scientists estimated it to be four billion years old. A reporter covering the Apollo 15 mission called it the Genesis Rock, a reference to the biblical creation story.

On their final day of lunar exploration, the astronauts drilled 10 feet (3 m) into the lunar surface and pulled out core samples. They set up equipment that would send data about the moon to Earth long after they were gone. Then Scott stood in front of the rover's television camera and performed one last experiment. He explained that he was going to test Galileo's theory that gravity acts equally on objects regardless of their mass. Because there is no air resistance on the moon, it was the perfect place to demonstrate the theory. "In my left hand, I have a feather; in my right hand, a hammer," said Scott. "I'll drop the two of them here and, hopefully, they'll hit the ground at the same time." Scott held out his arms and dropped the feather and the hammer. They hit the ground at the same time. "How about that!" Scott said. "Nothing like a little science on the Moon."

Scott and Irwin packed their samples, closed the lunar module hatch, and blasted off from the moon. They joined Worden in the command module and headed back to Earth. As Apollo 15 came through the fluffy clouds drifting over the Pacific Ocean, one of the three orange-and-white parachutes holding the command module only partially inflated. The cone plunged into the ocean with a mighty splash. But the astronauts weren't hurt. They emerged smiling and happy.

APOLLO 16—KEN MATTINGLY'S TURN

Ken Mattingly, bumped from the Apollo 13 mission because of his exposure to measles, was given another chance to go to space. On April 16, 1972, he flew as the command module pilot on Apollo 16. John Young was the mission commander, and Charlie Duke was the lunar module pilot. Apollo 16's landing site was the Descartes Highlands. Scientists hoped the astronauts would find evidence of recent volcanic activity in the hilly area.

The flight went smoothly until the astronauts reached the moon and prepared to land. The command module and the lunar module undocked and separated. As the spacecraft orbited the moon, the command module started to shake. Mattingly changed some settings, but the spacecraft still shook. Mission control delayed the landing. If the steering system on the command module failed, the spacecraft could start tumbling. It would not be able to dock with the lunar module for the trip back to Earth, and all three astronauts would be lost.

While mission control investigated, the command module and the lunar module circled the moon in formation. For hours, the crew waited anxiously for a decision from Houston. After their sixteenth orbit, mission control told Mattingly that the engine might shake, but he would be able to control it. The crew could proceed with the landing. The command module continued to orbit, and the lunar module landed. They were six hours behind schedule, but Young and Duke were on the moon.

The next morning, Young and Duke put on their space suits and prepared for their first moonwalk. "Hot dog, is this great!" said Duke as he hopped down the lunar module ladder.

Astronaut Ken Mattingly

"That first foot on the lunar surface is super." The astronauts set up experiments, drove the rover to various craters, and took samples. They brought back more than 200 pounds (91 kg) of samples but did not find any recent volcanic rock. Instead, their mission provided evidence that the moon was shaped by eons of meteorite bombardment. When the astronauts were ready to head back to Earth, Young drove the rover away from the lunar module and pointed its television camera toward the spacecraft. Then he walked back to the spacecraft and prepared to take off. Flight controllers at mission control captured the liftoff from the moon on live TV.

From lunar orbit, the astronauts launched a subsatellite. The small satellite circled the moon for thirty-four days and sent information about its mass, gravity field, and magnetic field back to Earth. On the coast back to Earth, Mattingly took an eighty-four-minute space walk. He floated to the service module and retrieved film cassettes from the Scientific Instrument Module. Equipment in this module had recorded all kinds of data about the lunar environment as Mattingly circled the moon. Scientists studied the information brought back from Apollo 16 for years.

APOLLO 17: THE LAST LUNAR LANDING

Apollo 17 launched on December 7, 1972. Gene Cernan, the flight commander, had flown on Gemini 9 and Apollo 10. It was the first spaceflight for Ron Evans, the command module pilot, and Harrison "Jack" Schmitt, the lunar module pilot. Rather than a degree in engineering and a military background (the typical astronaut background), Schmitt earned a PhD in geology from Harvard University. He completed a year of flight training and became a jet pilot before he was considered for spaceflight. Then he trained as an astronaut. Schmitt was the first scientist-astronaut to explore the moon.

The Apollo 17 landing site was a mountainous area, Taurus-Littrow. The area was thick with craters and rich in

Scientist and astronaut Jack Schmitt, lunar module pilot, retrieves samples from the lunar surface for study.

geological wonders. Boulders that had been flung out of the craters were strewn around the area. Scientists believed the highlands contained rocks both older and younger than those found on other missions, and so they hoped Apollo 17 would answer questions about how and when the moon had formed.

Cernan and Schmitt explored the lunar surface. Evans conducted experiments from lunar orbit. On the first day, Cernan's hammer snagged the right rear fender of the rover and tore off the thin material. When the men drove to their geology sites, clouds of moondust rained down on them. The dust threatened to clog the rover's gears and damage scientific instruments. It also put the astronauts in danger. As moondust turned their white space suits black, the dark color absorbed the sun's intense heat. The men had to brush off the abrasive grit, which had worked its way into every nook and cranny, before they entered the lunar module for the night.

In Houston, while the men on the moon slept, NASA engineers worked out a fix for the rover's fender—a replacement fender. The next morning, astronaut John Young explained to the crew how to fashion the fender from four laminated lunar surface maps, duct tape, and lamp clamps. Cernan and Schmitt mounted the fender on the rover and attached it with the clamps. It worked, and the second day of lunar exploration began.

When the mission was finished, Cernan pulled the makeshift fender off the rover and brought it back to Earth. It was displayed at the Smithsonian National Air and Space Museum in Washington, DC. Cernan and Schmitt drove in the lunar rover for more than an hour to South Massif. As Cernan darted past craters and swerved around boulders, Schmitt described the landscape to the scientists in Houston. The explorers took many bags of samples and then cruised to the next crater on their list and the next. At Shorty, a deep crater littered with rocks, Schmitt found streaks of orange moondust. Everything else they had found was light gray, dark gray, or tan. This was bright orange.

The astronauts hoped the orange soil would be proof of recent volcanic activity on the moon. The men carefully bagged samples of the orange dust. Scientists later confirmed that an explosive volcanic eruption created the soil, but tests showed it occurred about 3.7 billion years ago.

The final day of lunar exploration lasted more than seven hours. Cernan and Schmitt drove to the opposite end of the Taurus-Littrow Valley, the North Massif. They took samples from a huge boulder that had rolled down the mountain and split into five pieces. They trudged up steep slopes and hammered out chunks of rocks until their arms and hands ached.

After they loaded the lunar module for the last time, the astronauts recorded a message for a group of young people in Houston. NASA had invited students from seventy countries to watch Apollo 17's final moonwalk. "One of the most significant things we can think about when we think about Apollo is that it has opened for us, 'for us,' being the world, a challenge of the future," said Cernan. "The door is now cracked, but the promise of the future lies in the young people, not just in America, but the

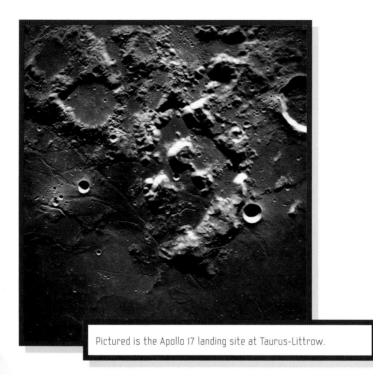

Pictured is the Apollo 17 landing site at Taurus-Littrow.

young people all over the world learning to live and learning to work together."

Schmitt handed Cernan a moon rock. "It's a rock composed of many fragments, of many sizes, and many shapes . . . that have grown together to become a cohesive rock, outlasting the nature of space, sort of living together in a very coherent, very peaceful manner. . . . We hope that this will be a symbol of what our feelings are, what the feelings of the Apollo Program are, and a symbol of mankind: that we can live in peace and harmony in the future."

Cernan uncovered a plaque attached to the portion of the lunar module that stayed on the moon. Two maps represented the world, the western half and the eastern half. Between the maps of Earth sat a small diagram of the moon with the landing sites of each Apollo mission shown. Cernan read the inscription on the plaque. "Here man completed his first exploration of the Moon,

December 1972 A.D. May the spirit of peace in which we came be reflected in the lives of all mankind." Each of the Apollo 17 astronauts and Nixon had signed the plaque.

The final Apollo mission broke every record of the lunar landing program. Its astronauts stayed on the moon longer, drove farther, collected more samples, set up more experiments, and took more photographs than any Apollo mission had. Their mission was also the smoothest and most trouble-free.

Apollo 17 marked the end of an era. No one has stepped on the moon since 1972. For some, the end brought relief. They hoped, instead, to spend space exploration dollars to wipe out poverty, social unrest, and many other problems in the United States and around the world. For others, the end of Apollo brought sadness and a time of reflection. "Of all humankind's achievements in the twentieth century . . . the one event that will dominate the history books a half a millennium from now will be our escape from our earthly environment and landing on the moon," said broadcast journalist Walter Cronkite.

After the Apollo program ended, NASA lacked a clearly defined goal for space exploration. Some people at the agency and in Congress wanted to focus on finding a way to reach and explore Mars. Others thought resources should be spent building reusable space shuttles. And still others thought building a space station was the top priority. Nixon cut NASA's budget. Unlike Kennedy, he did not lay out a clear-cut goal for space exploration that NASA could embrace.

If space exploration was going to continue, NASA needed a new vision.

10

APOLLO'S LEGACY

SPACE IS FOR EVERYBODY. IT'S NOT JUST FOR A FEW PEOPLE IN SCIENCE OR MATH, OR FOR A SELECT GROUP OF ASTRONAUTS. THAT'S OUR NEW FRONTIER OUT THERE.

—CHRISTA MCAULIFFE, TEACHER AND *CHALLENGER* ASTRONAUT

After the Apollo program ended, NASA launched a series of unmanned spacecraft to explore the solar system. Robot spacecraft flew by and collected data from Mercury, Mars, Neptune, Jupiter, and Saturn. NASA also built a space station as a science and engineering laboratory.

SKYLAB

NASA launched Skylab, America's first space station, on May 14, 1973, with one of the leftover Saturn V rockets from the Apollo program. Skylab orbited Earth while three-man crews tested how weightlessness affected their muscles and body systems for extended periods. They also conducted scientific experiments in solar astronomy, life sciences, and Earth studies. The first team of astronauts lived and worked on the space station for twenty-eight days. The second crew spent fifty-nine days in space, and the third crew lived in space for eighty-four days. Besides the crew, Skylab

The three Skylab crews conducted nearly three hundred experiments in space.

carried mice, spiders, and fish into space to test the effects of weightlessness on animals.

FROM COMPETITION TO COOPERATION

The space race began as a competition between the United States and the Soviet Union. It ended in a spirit of cooperation between the two nations. The Apollo-Soyuz Test Project brought the two superpowers together in the vastness of space. On July 17, 1975, three American astronauts in the final Apollo command module met two Soviet cosmonauts in a Soyuz spacecraft and flew in orbit around Earth.

The spacecraft moved close to each other, and their crews took photographs. Then Apollo commander Thomas Stafford guided the Apollo command module to the Soyuz spacecraft and docked, joining the spacecraft together. A few minutes later, hatches opened, and astronauts and cosmonauts shook hands. It was the beginning of a new era of unity in space. "We were a little of a spark or a foot in the door that started better communications," said American astronaut Vance Brand.

SPACE SHUTTLES

NASA spent the rest of the 1970s and 1980s creating the space shuttle program. Designed to lower the cost of getting to space, space shuttles were reusable spacecraft. A cross between a spacecraft

Astronaut Thomas P. Stafford and cosmonaut Alexei A. Leonov in the hatchway between the Apollo docking module and the Soyuz orbital module during the joint US-USSR Apollo-Soyuz Test Project. The spacecraft spent about forty-seven hours joined together as they orbited Earth.

and a jet plane, space shuttles launched from Earth like a rocket and glided back to the ground with wings like an airplane. Shuttles ferried astronauts and supplies to and from space stations orbiting Earth. They also launched, repaired, and recovered satellites. A fleet of five space shuttle crafts flew 135 missions from April 1981 to July 2011. The program pushed the boundaries of space exploration. Thousands of people worked to create the technologies needed for the space shuttle program.

The space shuttle *Columbia* lifts off from launchpad 39A on January 16, 2003.

The space shuttle program saw tragedy as well as success. On January 28, 1986, the space shuttle *Challenger* exploded shortly after liftoff. All seven crew members died, including Christa McAuliffe, the first teacher chosen to fly into space. NASA put a hold on space shuttle flights for nearly three years and made safety improvements to the spacecraft. With the launch of *Discovery* on September 29, 1988, shuttle missions resumed. But on February 1, 2003, a second disaster struck the program when the shuttle *Columbia* broke apart during reentry and killed its seven-person crew.

INTERNATIONAL SPACE STATION

The space shuttle program made it possible for NASA to help build the largest structure in space, the International Space Station (ISS). The United States and Russia worked together to build the ISS. The bulk of the construction took place between 1998 and 2011, and updates to the structure continued as needed. The ISS is the size of a football field. Each section was built on Earth. Space shuttles carried the pieces into space, and astronauts put them together during space walks as the station orbited Earth. Robot arms helped astronauts move modules and equipment into the correct position.

The ISS is a giant research laboratory. Astronauts from eighteen countries have lived and worked together on the ISS to explore the solar system. They conduct experiments on plants, animals, and themselves. They study and predict weather patterns on Earth, monitor natural resources, and assess crop yields. They also test new products, such as espresso machines and 3D printers. Besides human astronauts, the ISS has a humanlike space robot on board. Robonaut flips switches and performs routine tasks while the astronauts sleep.

The sun powers the ISS. Solar panels convert the sun's energy to electricity. Docking ports act like car garages and allow astronauts from all around the world to attach their spacecraft to the ISS and stay awhile. Most astronauts work in the ISS for six months at a time. In 2015 to 2016, NASA astronaut Scott Kelly and Russian cosmonaut Mikhail Kornienko lived and worked together

The International Space Station, photographed by a crew member on board the space shuttle *Atlantis* on May 23, 2010

New Inventions for Living in Space

NASA developed many new products to enable astronauts to live comfortably in a weightless environment. They built special showers, toilets, sleeping bags, and kitchen tools to work in microgravity. They also designed special exercise equipment for use in space. Exercising in space is a top priority for astronauts. On Earth, gravity provides resistance for our muscles and bones. But in microgravity, there is no resistance. Without exercise, astronauts' bones would become fragile and their muscles would weaken. To prevent bone and muscle loss, astronauts work out at least two hours a day. They ride a bicycle, jog on a treadmill, and work out on resistance equipment similar to a weight-lifting machine on Earth.

Astronauts exercise every day to stay fit and preserve their bones and muscles while they live and work in space. Alexander Gerst, a German European Space Agency astronaut, works out on the International Space Station's fitness bike in 2014.

on the ISS for nearly a year. Astronauts are scheduled to live and work on the ISS until at least 2024.

The ISS costs the United States between $3 and 4 billion per year to operate. NASA is working with commercial space companies such as SpaceX to develop vehicles to transport US astronauts and supplies to the ISS and other destinations in low-Earth orbit. This would free up funds for NASA to explore deep space and plan expeditions back to the moon and to Mars.

A BOOK AND A FILM

In the 1990s, Lovell wrote his autobiography. He worked with science writer Jeffrey Kluger to chronicle his life as an astronaut and his path to that career. A new generation had grown up with little knowledge of his harrowing journey on Apollo 13. Lovell wanted to share the story from the view of someone who'd been there. The book, *Lost Moon: The Perilous Voyage of Apollo 13*, later became the basis of a film. Director Ron Howard acquired the rights to turn Lovell's book into *Apollo 13*, a blockbuster motion picture starring Tom Hanks.

Howard, the actors, and the film crew worked closely with NASA to make the film as authentic as possible. They built a replica of mission control in Hollywood. They borrowed NASA's KC-135 airplane, jokingly known as the vomit comet, for some of the scenes of weightlessness. Filming was tricky in the small space. Actors, cameras, and set pieces all floated. Howard had to film tiny slices at a time and then combine them for the final film. For the splashdown scene, the film crew built a model of the command module and dropped it into the ocean from a helicopter. Released in 1995, *Apollo 13* was a box office hit and won two Academy Awards.

BENEFITS FOR ALL

Space exploration has generated countless benefits for people around the globe. Laptop computers, cell phones, and the internet all use materials and processes developed for the space program.

THE HUBBLE SPACE TELESCOPE

On April 24, 1990, the Space Shuttle *Discovery* launched the Hubble Space Telescope into Earth orbit. This powerful telescope sits above the atmosphere and has a clear view of stars, planets, and galaxies. Hubble explores the universe twenty-four hours a day, 365 days a year. Hundreds of scientists, engineers, and technicians on the ground operate the telescope and monitor its health. The sun powers Hubble. It takes pictures of the cosmos as it whirls around Earth at 18,000 miles (28,968 km) per hour. The telescope has made more than 1.3 million observations, and its photographs have expanded our understanding of the universe. Astronomers using Hubble data have published more than sixteen thousand scientific papers, making the Hubble Space Telescope one of the most productive scientific instruments ever built.

On the first servicing mission to the Hubble Space Telescope, astronauts installed a set of specialized lenses to correct the flawed main mirror in the telescope.

The Hubble Space Telescope captured this image of the Sombrero galaxy, located 28 million light-years from Earth.

Personal entertainment devices and tablets are also possible because of the space age. Even the music we listen to on mobile devices has been translated into digital data, a technique first used in spaceflights.

The space program has brought important breakthroughs in health and medicine. Tools for diagnosing diseases, such as digital X-rays, CAT scans, and implantable heart monitors, use technology first built for use in space. Ear thermometers allow doctors to measure quickly and accurately the temperature of infants and critically ill patients. Improved artificial limbs and heart pumps for patients awaiting a heart transplant have improved the quality of life for thousands of people. Light-emitting diodes (LEDs) developed at NASA are being used by the US military for relieving muscle and joint pain in soldiers. LED technology can relieve pain in bone marrow transplant patients and people suffering from multiple sclerosis, diabetes, and Parkinson's disease.

Many products used in homes, schools, and offices were developed due to the space program. Water-purification systems, smoke detectors, and fire-resistant building materials make life safer on Earth. Firefighters wear protective suits made from fabric first used in space suits. They also carry lightweight breathing devices to protect them from smoke inhalation injuries. Temper foam, or memory foam, is used in mattresses, cars, football helmets, and furniture. Baby formula contains a nutrient discovered through NASA research. Athletic shoes, wireless headsets, solar panels, and panoramic camera technology all have roots in the economy of space.

Satellite technology is another benefit of the space program. The satellites that make up the Global Positioning System (GPS) allow us to navigate our world. Weather satellites send images and data about Earth's atmosphere to meteorologists. The information helps forecasters predict dangerous storms. Satellites also collect images of Earth's surface. This information helps scientists understand how global warming and other environmental concerns are changing our planet. And satellites provide data that scientists use to protect wildlife, manage crops, and conserve natural resources.

The space program has led to innovations in nearly every aspect of life. But Earth is not alone in the solar system. Events outside our planet are impacting its future. Space exploration will continue to make new discoveries that will improve life on Earth and expand our knowledge of the universe.

WHAT'S NEXT?

A new era of space travel is on the horizon. Private companies are working on launch systems to propel spacecraft into orbit and beyond. The US Air Force has awarded launch service agreements to Blue Origin, founded by Amazon CEO Jeff Bezos; Northrop Grumman Innovation Systems; and United Launch Alliance. Each company is developing a domestic launch system prototype. The air force will review the designs and select two as national space launch service providers.

Through new public-private partnerships, the space community is committed to providing safe, reliable access to space for the nation. Private companies, such as SpaceX and Virgin Galactic, plan to offer commercial spaceflights for customers with lots of vacation money. NASA is working with these companies to make sure their spacecraft meet NASA's rigorous safety standards. With private companies competing to handle short spaceflights, NASA is setting its sights on longer manned missions to the moon and to Mars.

Plans are underway for a lunar-orbiting station, the Lunar Orbiting Platform – Gateway, to pave the way for a lunar landing by 2024. Future missions will return US astronauts to the surface of the moon for extended exploration and study. NASA will use the knowledge gained from those missions to help with the next goal: landing astronauts on Mars.

Scientists are learning more about the Red Planet every day, thanks to *InSight*, NASA's Mars probe, which landed on Mars in November 2018. For the first time in history, scientists are learning

Hitching a Ride

After the space shuttle program ended in 2011, US astronauts and cargo traveled to the ISS riding on Russian Soyuz spacecraft. US astronauts trained in Russia so they would be able to operate the unfamiliar spacecraft. SpaceX and other private US companies are taking over the job of ferrying supplies, equipment, and people to the ISS.

SpaceX, the private space company founded by entrepreneur Elon Musk, began carrying cargo and supplies to and from the ISS in 2012. Soon SpaceX will begin carrying astronauts as well. SpaceX's Crew Dragon spacecraft can carry up to seven astronauts into low-Earth orbit. It includes a life-support system, an emergency-escape system, touch-screen displays, windows, and other passenger-related equipment.

Another private space company, Bigelow Aerospace, is developing a line of space stations that scientists can use for research. According

Private companies like SpaceX and Bigelow Aerospace are taking over the job of ferrying people and supplies into low-Earth orbit, freeing NASA to develop missions to the moon and to Mars.

to Robert Bigelow, founder and president of Bigelow, its space stations would be much cheaper to operate than the ISS. One Bigelow habitat, called the Bigelow Expandable Activity Module, connects to the ISS. Bigelow is also working on plans to offer space-bound travelers low-orbit hotels and other forms of space tourism.

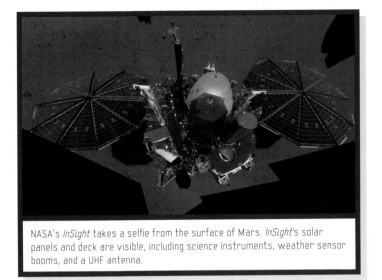

NASA's *InSight* takes a selfie from the surface of Mars. *InSight*'s solar panels and deck are visible, including science instruments, weather sensor booms, and a UHF antenna.

about the inner structure of Mars. This knowledge is helping them plan the safest way to land astronauts on the Red Planet. It may also help scientists learn more about our own planet's history and future.

To meet these ambitious goals, thousands of creative people will need to work together. Scientists, mathematicians, technology experts, engineers, and dreamers all have a place in the twenty-first century's space age. Unlike the space race of the 1960s, women will play key roles in every area of discovery as astronauts, scientists, flight controllers, and engineers. This new space age will be built on the foundation of the Apollo program. Apollo proved humanity could explore the universe beyond Earth. It revealed a future as rich in possibilities as space itself.

It's been fifty years since Apollo 13 splashed down in the Pacific Ocean. Remembering the triumph of that perilous voyage reminds us that any problem, even the most difficult problem, can be solved by ordinary people working together to reach a common goal. When machines break and technology fails, human ingenuity, hard work, and boldness turn failure into success.

Who knows what challenges the future will hold? Looking back on Apollo 13, we can be confident that whatever they are, we can solve them together.

OCTOBER 4, 1957	The Soviet Union launches *Sputnik I*, the world's first satellite.
OCTOBER 1, 1958	NASA officially begins operations.
APRIL 12, 1961	Russian cosmonaut Yuri Gagarin orbits Earth in *Vostok I*.
MAY 5, 1961	Alan Shepard becomes the first American in space.
JULY 21, 1961	Gus Grissom pilots *Liberty Bell 7* in a suborbital flight.
FEBRUARY 20, 1962	John Glenn becomes the first American to orbit Earth.
JUNE 16, 1963	Valentina Tereshkova of the Soviet Union becomes the first woman in space.
MARCH 18, 1965	Alexei Leonov of the Soviet Union is the first person to venture outside a spacecraft wearing a space suit.
MARCH 23, 1965–NOVEMBER 15, 1966	Project Gemini spaceflights test long-duration flights, rendezvous and docking with other spacecraft, and space walks.
JANUARY 27, 1967	The Apollo 1 fire in the training spacecraft kills Gus Grissom, Roger Chaffee, and Ed White.
OCTOBER 11–22, 1968	Apollo 7 is the first manned spaceflight to orbit Earth in the newly designed Apollo spacecraft.
DECEMBER 21–27, 1968	Apollo 8 becomes the first piloted flight to orbit the moon.

MARCH 3-13, 1969	Apollo 9 completes the first manned test of the lunar module in Earth orbit to rendezvous and dock with the command module.
MAY 18-26, 1969	Apollo 10 becomes the first manned test of the lunar module in lunar orbit to rendezvous and dock with the command module.
JULY 16-24, 1969	Apollo 11 completes the first lunar landing at the Sea of Tranquility.
NOVEMBER 14-24, 1969	Apollo 12 completes the second lunar landing at the Ocean of Storms. The precision landing is accomplished and scientific observation conducted from lunar orbit.
APRIL 11, 1970	Apollo 13 is launched.
APRIL 13, 1970	Astronauts Lovell, Haise, and Swigert broadcast a TV show from Apollo 13.
	Swigert flips a switch to stir the oxygen tanks.
	An explosion in oxygen tank 2 cripples the Apollo 13 spacecraft.
	The astronauts leave the command module *Odyssey* and move into the lunar module *Aquarius*.
APRIL 14, 1970	A midcourse correction is made to travel around the moon.
	A long burn is made to speed up the return to Earth.

APRIL 15, 1970	Lovell, Haise, and Swigert make lithium hydroxide canisters to filter dangerous carbon dioxide.
	A midcourse correction is made to adjust the trajectory for reentry.
APRIL 16, 1970	Ken Mattingly reads the command module power-up checklist to Jack Swigert.
APRIL 17, 1970	A midcourse correction fine-tunes the reentry trajectory.
	Lovell, Haise, and Swigert jettison the service module.
	Lovell, Haise, and Swigert jettison the lunar module.
	Apollo 13 splashes down in the Pacific Ocean.
JANUARY 31–FEBRUARY 9, 1971	Apollo 14 completes the first lunar landing on lunar highlands at Fra Mauro.
JULY 26–AUGUST 7, 1971	Apollo 15 completes a Hadley Rille lunar landing. It is the first moon landing with a lunar rover and first scientific observation platform operated from lunar orbit.
APRIL 16–27, 1972	Apollo 16 completes a Descartes Highlands lunar landing. Astronauts search for lunar volcanoes and explore the moon's central highlands for three days.
DECEMBER 7–19, 1972	Apollo 17 completes the final lunar landing at Taurus-Littrow. The mission is the most extensive lunar exploration ever accomplished.

MAY 14, 1973	NASA launches Skylab, America's first space station.
JULY 17, 1975	The Apollo-Soyuz Test Project occurs. The US Apollo spacecraft docks with the Soviet Soyuz spacecraft.
APRIL 12, 1981– JULY 21, 2011	Five space shuttles fly 135 missions into Earth orbit.
JUNE 18, 1983	Sally Ride becomes the first American woman in space.
AUGUST 30, 1983	Guion Bluford becomes the first African American in space.
JANUARY 28, 1986	Space shuttle *Challenger* explodes shortly after liftoff and kills the seven-person crew.
APRIL 24, 1990	Space shuttle *Discovery* launches the Hubble Space Telescope into Earth orbit.
SEPTEMBER 12, 1992	Mae Jemison becomes the first African American woman in space.
JUNE 30, 1995	The film *Apollo 13* is released.
1998–2011	The United States and Russia build the International Space Station.
FEBRUARY 1, 2003	Space shuttle *Columbia* breaks apart during reentry and kills the seven-person crew.
SEPTEMBER 17, 2018	Holly Ridings becomes the first female chief flight director at the Johnson Space Center in Houston, Texas.
NOVEMBER 26, 2018	The Mars probe *InSight* lands on Mars.
AUGUST 23, 2019	NASA's Deep Space Atomic Clock begins a one-year test.

Glossary

alignment: a spacecraft's position in relation to other objects in space

altitude: the height of an object above a given planet or moon

attitude: a spacecraft's orientation in space

burn: a short firing of a rocket engine to change a spacecraft's course or flight path

carbon dioxide: a colorless gas exhaled during breathing. Too much carbon dioxide in a confined area will cause someone to get sick.

command module: the cone-shaped Apollo 13 spacecraft called *Odyssey.* It contained the crew compartment, instrument panels, and heat shield.

fuel cell: a device in the service module that mixed oxygen and hydrogen to make electricity and water

gravity: the force that pulls everything toward a large object such as a planet or moon

hatch: a doorway in a spacecraft

heat shield: the part of a spacecraft that protects the rest of the craft from the heat of reentering Earth's atmosphere

jettison: to release

lithium hydroxide canisters: air scrubbers that remove carbon dioxide from the spacecraft and purify the air

lunar module: the spider-shaped Apollo 13 spacecraft called *Aquarius.* It was the only part of the spacecraft designed to land on the moon. The Apollo 13 crew used it as a lifeboat on their trip back to Earth.

midcourse correction: burning a spacecraft's engine on the way to or from the moon to place it on the correct flight path

mission control: NASA flight controllers who monitor and manage spaceflights

orbit: to travel in an ellipse around a planet or moon

oxygen: a gas that humans breathe

passive thermal control roll: a maneuver to slowly roll a spacecraft so it doesn't get too hot on the part facing the sun or too cold on the part facing away from the sun

recovery ship: a ship sent to where a manned spacecraft is expected to land

reentry: to come back into Earth's atmosphere from space

service module: attached to the command module, the part of the spacecraft that looks like a giant tin can. It contains oxygen, water, heat, and electrical power for the spacecraft.

simulator: a machine astronauts use on the ground at NASA to train for piloting spacecraft

thruster: a small engine used to adjust the position or flight path of a spacecraft

trajectory: the path of an object moving through space

Source Notes

4   Francis French and Colin Burgess, *Into That Silent Sea: Trailblazers of the Space Era, 1961–1965* (Lincoln: University of Nebraska Press, 2007), 127.

8   David Woods, Alexandr Turhanov, and Lennox J. Waugh, "Day 3: Before the Storm," 046:43:38," NASA, *Apollo 13 Flight Journal*, last modified February 17, 2017, https://history.nasa.gov/afj/ap13fj/07day3-before-the -storm.html.

8   Andrew Chaikin, *A Man on the Moon: The Voyages of the Apollo Astronauts* (New York: Penguin Books, 2007), 290.

9   David Woods, Alexandr Turhanov, and Lennox J. Waugh, "Day 3: 'Houston, We've Had a Problem," 055:55:19–055:55:35, NASA, *Apollo 13 Flight Journal*, last modified May 30, 2017, https://history.nasa.gov/afj/ap13fj/08day3 -problem.html.

10   Gerhard Peters and John T. Woolley, "John F. Kennedy Address at Rice University in Houston on the Nation's Space Effort, September 12, 1962," *The American Presidency Project*, accessed July 12, 2018, http:// www.presidency.ucsb.edu/node/236798.

14   French and Burgess, *Into That Silent Sea*, 41.

14–15   French and Burgess, 56.

15   M. Scott Carpenter, L. Gordon Cooper Jr., John H. Glenn Jr., Virgil I. Grissom, Walter M. Schirra Jr., Alan B. Shepard Jr., and Donald K. Slayton, *We Seven*, rev. ed. (1990; repr., New York: Simon & Schuster Pbks., 2010), 21.

15   Carpenter, Cooper, Glenn, Grissom, Schirra, Shepard, and Slayton, 21.

15   Gerhard Peters and John T. Woolley, "John F. Kennedy Special Message to the Congress on Urgent National Needs, May 25, 1961," *The American Presidency Project*, accessed July 12, 2018, http://www.presidency.ucsb .edu/node/234560.

16   Carpenter, Cooper, Glenn, Grissom, Schirra, Shepard, and Slayton, *We Seven*, 226.

19   French and Burgess, *Into That Silent Sea*, 190.

21   Bob Granath, NASA, "Gemini IV: Learning to Walk in Space," NASA.gov, December 28, 2017, https://www.nasa.gov/feature/gemini-iv-learning-to -walk-in-space.

22   Lynn M. Homan and Thomas Reilly, *Historic Journeys into Space* (Charleston, SC: Arcadia, 2000), 45.

23   Gene Kranz, *Failure Is Not an Option: Mission Control from Mercury to Apollo 13 and Beyond* (New York: Simon & Schuster, 2000), 202–203.

23   Eric M. Jones, "The First Lunar Landing," 102:45:58," NASA, *Apollo 11 Lunar Surface Journal*, May 10, 2018, https://www.hq.nasa.gov/alsj/a11/AS11_PAO.PDF.

23   Eric M. Jones, "One Small Step," 109:24:23, NASA, *Apollo 11 Lunar Surface Journal*, April 18, 2018, https://www.hq.nasa.gov/alsj/a11/AS11_PAO.PDF.

23   Brooke Boen, NASA, "Apollo 11 Plaque Left on the Moon," NASA, July 16, 2009, https://www.nasa.gov/centers/marshall/moonmars/apollo40/apollo11_plaque.html.

28   Sy Liebergot, *Apollo EECOM: Journey of a Lifetime* (Burlington, ONT: Apogee Books, 2006), 138.

35   Woods, Turhanov, and Waugh, "Day 3: 'Houston, We've Had a Problem,'" 056:09:07–056:09:29, NASA, *Apollo 13 Flight Journal*, last modified May 30, 2017, https://history.nasa.gov/afj/ap13fj/08day3-problem.html.

36   Stephen Cass, "Apollo 13, We Have a Solution," *IEEE Spectrum*, April 1, 2005, https://spectrum.ieee.org/tech-history/space-age/apollo-13-we-have-a-solution.

35   Liebergot, *Apollo*, 112.

36   Kranz, *Failure Is Not an Option*, 315.

36   Woods, Turhanov, and Waugh, "Day 3: 'Houston, We've Had a Problem,'" 056:28:06.

38   David Woods, Alexandr Turhanov, and Lennox J. Waugh, "Day 3: Aquarius becomes a lifeboat, 058:04:03," NASA, *Apollo 13 Flight Journal*, last modified February 2, 2017, https://history.nasa.gov/afj/ap13fj/09day3-lifeboat.html.

39   Chaikin, *A Man on the Moon*, 301.

39   Woods, Turhanov, and Waugh, "Day 3: *Aquarius* Becomes a Lifeboat," 058:40:12–058:40:22.

40   Martin Waldron, "Flight Director Is Making the Decisions," *New York Times*, April 16, 1970.

44   Stephen Cass, "Apollo 13, We Have a Solution: Part 2," *IEEE Spectrum*, April 1, 2005, https://spectrum.ieee.org/tech-history/space-age/apollo-13-we-have-a-solution-part-2.

45   David Woods, Alexandr Turhanov, and Lennox J. Waugh, "Day 3: Free Return," 060:24:08, NASA, *Apollo 13 Flight Journal*, last modified June 12, 2017, https://history.nasa.gov/afj/ap13fj/10day3-free-return.html.

47   Woods, Turhanov, and Waugh, 066:08:35-066:08:41.

50   John Noble Wilford, "Target Is Pacific," *New York Times*, April 15, 1970.

51   Jim Lovell and Jeffrey Kluger, *Apollo 13*, rev. ed. (2006; previously published as *Lost Moon*. Boston: Mariner Books, 1994), 213.

52   Rob Garner, "Dr. Robert H. Goddard, American Rocketry Pioneer," NASA, August 3, 2017, https://www.nasa.gov/centers/goddard/about/history /dr_goddard.html.

54   David Woods, Alexandr Turhanov, and Lennox J. Waugh, "Day 4: Approaching the Moon," 073:46:52-073:47:10, NASA, *Apollo 13 Flight Journal*, last modified February 17, 2017, https://history.nasa.gov/afj /ap13fj/12day4-approach-moon.html.

54   Charles R. Pellegrino and Joshua Stoff, *Chariots for Apollo: The Making of the Lunar Module* (New York: Atheneum, 1985), 188.

54   Lovell and Kluger, *Apollo 13*, 240.

55   David Woods, Alexandr Turhanov, and Lennox J. Waugh, "Day 4: Leaving the Moon," 078:02:44, NASA, *Apollo 13 Flight Journal*, last modified February 17, 2017, https://history.nasa.gov/afj/ap13fj/13day4-leaving-moon .html.

56   Woods, Turhanov, and Waugh, 079:33:13–079:33:18.

57   Pellegrino and Stoff, *Chariots for Apollo*, 202.

58   Woods, Turhanov, and Waugh, "Day 4: Leaving the Moon," 080:22:13.

60   Pellegrino and Stoff, *Chariots for Apollo*, 198.

61   Stephen Cass, "Apollo 13, We Have a Solution: Part 3," *IEEE Spectrum*, April 1, 2005, https://spectrum.ieee.org/tech-history/space-age/apollo-13 -we-have-a-solution-part-3.

63   David Woods, Alexandr Turhanov, and Lennox J. Waugh, "Apollo 13 Flight Journal Fifth Day," 108:54:37, NASA, *Apollo 13 Flight Journal Fifth Day*, last modified August 27, 2018, (forthcoming), transcript to author from David Woods.

64   David Woods, Alexandr Turhanov, and Lennox J. Waugh, "Apollo 13 Flight Journal Sixth Day," 122:57:13–122:57:22, NASA, *Apollo 13 Flight Journal Sixth Day*, last modified August 27, 2018, (forthcoming), transcript to author from David Woods.

67   Woods, Turhanov, and Waugh, "Apollo 13 Flight Journal Fifth Day," 111:05:09.

68–69   Woods, Turhanov, and Waugh, 118:44:45–118:45:05."

69   Woods, Turhanov, and Waugh, "Apollo 13 Flight Journal Sixth Day," 127:59:13–128:00:40.

69   Woods, Turhanov, and Waugh, 128:00:55–128:01:04.

70   Edgar M. Cortright, ed., *Apollo: Expeditions to the Moon* (Mineola, NY: Dover, 2009), 262.

71   Woods, Turhanov, and Waugh, "Apollo 13 Flight Journal Sixth Day," 135:46:52.

71   Woods, Turhanov, and Waugh, 133:22:08–133:23:29.

73   Woods, Turhanov, and Waugh, 138:04:46–138:09:09.

75   Woods, Turhanov, and Waugh, 140:54:28–140:54:35.

76   Woods, Turhanov, and Waugh, 141:30:05.

77   Martin Waldron, "Applause, Cigars and Champagne Toasts Greet Capsule's Landing," *New York Times*, April 18, 1970.

78   Woods, Turhanov, and Waugh, "Apollo 13 Flight Journal Sixth Day," 142:22:28–142:22:36.

79–80   Woods, Turhanov, and Waugh, 142:46:03–142:46:12.

80   Waldron, "Applause, Cigars and Champagne."

80   Waldron.

82   Gerhard Peters and John T. Woolley, "Richard Nixon: Remarks Announcing Plans to Award the Presidential Medal of Freedom to Apollo 13 Astronauts and Mission Operations Team, April 17, 1970," *The American Presidency Project*, accessed October 17, 2018, http://www.presidency.ucsb.edu /node/241042.

84   Homan and Reilly, *Historic Journeys*, 71.

85–86   Gerhard Peters and John T. Woolley, "Richard Nixon, Remarks on Presenting the Presidential Medal of Freedom to Apollo 13 Mission Operations Team in Houston, April 18, 1970," *The American Presidency Project*, accessed July 12, 2018, https://www.presidency.ucsb.edu /node/241054.

86–87   Gerhard Peters and John T. Woolley, "Richard Nixon: Remarks on Presenting Presidential Medal of Freedom to Apollo 13 Astronauts in Honolulu, April 18, 1970," *The American Presidency Project*, accessed October 17, 2018, http://www.presidency.ucsb.edu/node/241069.

87   Peters and Woolley.

88   John Noble Wilford, "Nixon Restates His Support of Space Effort," New York Times, April 20, 1970.

88   Lloyd Mathews, "Astronauts Telling of Ordeal: Welcomed Back Here by 5000," *Houston Chronicle*, April 20, 1970.

88   Mathews.

88   "Apollo 13 Post Flight Press Conference (1970)," YouTube video, 1:15:54,
      posted by "AIRBOYD," November 25, 2012, https://www.youtube.com
      /watch?v=IMMw2QIHBLs&t=31s.

88   "Apollo 13 Post Flight Press Conference."

88   "Apollo 13 Post Flight Press Conference."

91   Edgar M. Cortright, "Report of Apollo 13 Review Board," National
      Aeronautics and Space Administration, April 21, 1970, 5–3, https://
      history.nasa.gov/afj/ap13fj/pdf/report-of-a13-review-board-19700615
      -19700076776.pdf.

96   French and Burgess, *Into That Silent Sea*, 162.

98   Eric M. Jones, "Deploying the Lunar Roving Vehicle," 119:55:45, NASA,
      Apollo 15 Lunar Surface Journal, last modified October 27, 2017, https://
      www.hq.nasa.gov/alsj/a15/a15.lrvdep.html.

99   Eric M. Jones, "Return to the LM," 123:33:39, NASA, *Apollo 15 Lunar
      Surface Journal*, last modified October 14, 2016, https://www.hq.nasa.gov
      /alsj/a15/a15.trvlm1.html.

100   Eric M. Jones, "The Hammer and the Feather,"167:22:06–167:23:30,
      NASA, *Apollo 15 Lunar Surface Journal*, last modified April 19, 2015,
      https://www.hq.nasa.gov/alsj/a15/a15.clsout3.html.

101–102 Eric M. Jones, "Back in the Briar Patch," 119:05:43–119:06:24, NASA,
      Apollo 16 Lunar Surface Journal, last modified December 7, 2012, https://
      www.hq.nasa.gov/alsj/a16/a16.eva1prelim.html.

104–105 Eric M. Jones, "EVA-3 Close-Out," 169:43:06, NASA, *Apollo 17 Lunar
      Surface Journal*, last modified October 12, 2016, https://www.hq.nasa.gov
      /alsj/a17/a17.clsout3.html.

105   Jones, 169:44:45.

106   Jones, 169:47:19.

106   Walter Cronkite, *A Reporter's Life* (New York: Alfred A. Knopf, 1996), 271.

107   Jerry Woodfill, "Space Quotes," *NASA Space Educators' Handbook*,
      February 15, 2000, https://er.jsc.nasa.gov/seh/quotes.html.

108   Jim Wilson, "Apollo-Soyuz; An Orbital Partnership Begins," NASA, last
      modified August 7, 2017, https://www.nasa.gov/topics/history/features
      /astp.html.

Selected Bibliography

"Apollo 13 Technical Crew Debriefing," Missions Operations Branch. NASA, April 24, 1970, https://www.hq.nasa.gov/alsj/a13/a13-techdebrief.pdf.

Atkinson, Nancy. "A Conversation with Apollo's Jim Lovell, Part 1: NASA's Future." Universe Today, September 23, 2010. https://www.universetoday.com/74302/a-conversation-with-apollos-jim-lovell-part-1-nasas-future.

———. "A Conversation with Apollo's Jim Lovell, Part 2: Looking Back." Universe Today, September 27, 2010. https://www.universetoday.com/74396/a-conversation-with-jim-lovell-part-2-looking-back.

Carpenter, M. Scott, L. Gordon Cooper Jr., John H. Glenn Jr., Virgil I. Grissom, Walter M. Schirra Jr., Alan B. Shepard Jr., and Donald K. Slayton. *We Seven.* Rev. ed. 1990. Reprint, New York: Simon & Schuster Pbks., 2010.

Cass, Stephen. "Apollo 13: We Have a Solution." *IEEE Spectrum*, April 1, 2005. https://spectrum.ieee.org/tech-history/space-age/apollo-13-we-have-a-solution.

———. "Apollo 13, We Have a Solution: Part 2." *IEEE Spectrum*, April 1, 2005. https://spectrum.ieee.org/tech-history/space-age/apollo-13-we-have-a-solution-part-2.

———. "Apollo 13, We Have a Solution: Part 3." *IEEE Spectrum*, April 1, 2005. https://spectrum.ieee.org/tech-history/space-age/apollo-13-we-have-a-solution-part-3.

Chaikin, Andrew. *A Man on the Moon: The Voyages of the Apollo Astronauts.* New York: Penguin Books, 2007.

Collins, Michael. *Carrying the Fire: An Astronaut's Journeys.* New York: Cooper Square, 2001.

Cooper, Henry S., Jr. *Thirteen: The Apollo Flight That Failed.* Baltimore: Johns Hopkins University Press, 1972.

Cortright, Edgar M., ed. *Apollo: Expeditions to the Moon.* Mineola, NY: Dover, 2009.

DeNooyer, Rush, Kirk Wolfinger, Gene Kranz, Christopher Kraft, and Robert Seamans. *Failure Is Not an Option.* New York: A & E Television Networks, 2003.

Earth to the Moon: Mercury, Gemini, Apollo Missions 1958 to 1972. Glendale, CA: Total Content Digital, 2017.

French, Francis, and Colin Burgess. *Into That Silent Sea: Trailblazers of the Space Era, 1961–1965.* Lincoln: University of Nebraska Press, 2007.

Godwin, Robert, ed. *Apollo 13: The NASA Mission Reports.* Burlington, ONT: Apogee Books, 2000.

Himmel, Eric, ed. *Apollo: Through the Eyes of the Astronauts.* New York: Abrams, 2009.

Homan, Lynn M., and Thomas Reilly. *Historic Journeys into Space.* Charleston, SC: Arcadia, 2000.

Howard, Ron, dir. *Apollo 13.* Universal CIty, CA: Universal Pictures and Imagine Entertainment, 1995.

Jones, Eric. *Apollo 11 Lunar Surface Journal.* NASA. Last modified March 26, 2019. https://www.hq.nasa.gov/alsj/a11/a11.html.

———. *Apollo 11 Lunar Surface Journal.* NASA, Last modified October 21, 2017, https://www.hq.nasa.gov/alsj/a14/a14.html.

———. *Apollo 11 Lunar Surface Journal.* NASA, Last modified May 16, 2017, https://www.hq.nasa.gov/alsj/a15/a15.html.

———. *Apollo 11 Lunar Surface Journal.* NASA, Last modified March 5, 2016, https://www.hq.nasa.gov/alsj/a16/a16.html.

———. *Apollo 11 Lunar Surface Journal.* NASA, Last modified December 18, 2015, https://www.hq.nasa.gov/alsj/a17/a17.html.

Kraft, Chris. *Flight: My Life in Mission Control.* New York: Dutton, 2001.

Kranz, Gene. *Failure Is Not an Option: Mission Control from Mercury to Apollo 13 and Beyond.* New York: Simon & Schuster, 2000.

Liebergot, Sy. *Apollo EECOM: Journey of a Lifetime.* Burlington, ONT: Apogee Books, 2006.

Lovell, Jim, and Jeffrey Kluger. *Apollo 13.* Rev. ed., 2006. Previously published as *Lost Moon.* Boston: Mariner Books, 1994.

Low, George M. "Report of Apollo 13 Review Board," NASA, April 21, 1970. https://history.nasa.gov/afj/ap13fj/pdf/report-of-a13-review-board-19700615 -19700076776.pdf

Man on the Moon with Walter Cronkite. Los Angeles: CBS News, Timeless Media Group, 2008.

Moore, Patrick. *The Apollo Story.* London: Revelation Films and Science Museum, 1995.

Murray, Charles, and Catherine Bly Cox. *Apollo: The Race to the Moon.* New York: Simon and Schuster, 1989.

Niel, Martin, dir. *Apollo 13: Houston, We've Had a Problem*. London: Revelation Films and Science Museum, 1995.

Pellegrino, Charles R., and Joshua Stoff. *Chariots for Apollo: The Making of the Lunar Module*. New York: Atheneum, 1985.

Petrone, Rocco A. "Apollo 13 Post Launch Mission Operation Report." NASA, April 28, 1970, https://www.hq.nasa.gov/alsj/a13/A13_MissionOpReport.pdf.

Pyle, Rod. *Destination Moon: The Apollo Missions in the Astronauts' Own Words*. New York: Harper Collins Books, 2005.

Reynolds, David West. *Apollo: The Epic Journey to the Moon, 1963–1972*. Minneapolis: Zenith, 2013.

Sington, David, dir. *In the Shadow of the Moon*. New York: Discovery Films, 2007.

Weaver, Elliot, and Zander Weaver, dir. *13 Factors That Saved Apollo 13*. Brighton, UK: Espresso TV, 2014.

Wiseman, Don, dir. *Apollo 13: The Complete Story, the Astronauts' Perspectives*. Houston, TX: A-V Corporation, 2017.

Woods, David, Alexandr Turhanov and Lennox J. Waugh. *Apollo 13 Flight Journal*. NASA. Last modified February 17, 2017. https://history.nasa.gov/afj/ap13fj /index.html.

Woods, David. *How Apollo Flew to the Moon*. Chichester, UK: Praxis, 2008.

Further Reading

Books

Aldrin, Buzz, and Marianne Dyson. *To the Moon and Back: My Apollo 11 Adventure*. Washington, DC: National Geographic Children's Books, 2018.

Chaikin, Andrew, Victoria Kohl, and Alan Bean. *Mission Control, This Is Apollo: The Story of the First Voyages to the Moon*. New York: Viking, 2009.

Dyson, Marianne J. *Home on the Moon: Living on a Space Frontier*. Washington, DC: National Geographic, 2003.

Hasday, Judy L. *The Apollo 13 Mission*. Philadelphia: Chelsea House, 2001.

Holden, Henry M. *Danger in Space: Surviving the Apollo 13 Disaster*. Berkeley Heights, NJ: Enslow, 2013.

Jones, Tom. *Ask the Astronaut: A Galaxy of Astonishing Answers to Your Questions on Spaceflight*. Washington, DC: Smithsonian Books, 2016.

Morgan, Ben, ed. *Space! The Universe as You've Never Seen It Before*. New York: DK, 2015.

Olson, Tod. *Lost in Outer Space: The Incredible Journey of Apollo 13*. New York: Scholastic, 2017.

O'Shaughnessy, Tam. *Sally Ride: A Photobiography of America's Pioneering Woman in Space*. New York: Roaring Brook, 2015.

Zoehfeld, Kathleen Weidner. *Apollo 13: How Three Brave Astronauts Survived a Space Disaster*. New York: Random House, 2015.

Websites

NASA: Apollo 13 Mission
https://www.nasa.gov/mission_pages/apollo/apollo-13
Learn more about the Apollo 13 crew on NASA's official mission
website.

NASA Astronaut Candidate Program
https://astronauts.nasa.gov/content/broch00.htm
Find out the qualifications and requirements for becoming an
astronaut.

NASA Kids' Club
https://www.nasa.gov/kidsclub/index.html
Test your rover-driving skills, find out who is on the space
station, and more.

NASA Space Educators' Handbook
https://er.jsc.nasa.gov/seh/seh.html
Search for and reference NASA resources using this online
encyclopedia.

NASA Space Place
https://spaceplace.nasa.gov/classroom-activities/en/
Use this site's activities to learn more about concepts related to
Earth and space.

Smithsonian National Air and Space Museum: Apollo Program
https://airandspace.si.edu/topics/apollo-program
Read recent articles about the equipment, technology, and
engineers that made the Apollo missions possible.

https://airandspace.si.edu/explore-and-learn/topics/apollo/apollo
-program/
Read detailed summaries of each Apollo mission.

Index

About the Author

Laura Edge loves to read, travel, dance, and watch football games. She also enjoys visiting NASA, near her home in Houston, Texas, where she has stood beside a Saturn V rocket, strolled through the Mission Control Center, and explored the astronaut-training facility with family and friends. Edge has taught reading, writing, math, and computer programming. She is the author of fifteen nonfiction books for children and is currently working on a picture book and a middle-grade novel.